CHARTER SCHOOLS

CHARTER SCHOOLS

THOMAS MURPHY (EDITOR)

Nova Science Publishers, Inc.
New York

Senior Editors: Susan Boriotti and Donna Dennis
Coordinating Editor: Tatiana Shohov
Office Manager: Annette Hellinger
Graphics: Wanda Serrano
Book Production: Matthew Kozlowski, Jonathan Rose and Jennifer Vogt
Circulation: Raymond Davis, Cathy DeGregory and Ave Maria Gonzalez
Communications and Acquisitions: Serge P. Shohov

Library of Congress Cataloging-in-Publication Data

Charter schools / [edited by] Thomas Murphy.
   p. cm.
   Includes index.
   ISBN 1-59033-196-6.
   1. Charter schools. I. Murphy, Thomas (Thomas Zacharaiah)

LB2806.36 .C535 2002
371.01—dc21

                                                 2001059623

Copyright © 2002 by Nova Science Publishers, Inc.
         227 Main Street, Suite 100
         Huntington, New York 11743
         Tele. 631-424-NOVA (6682)   Fax 631-425-5933
         E Mail: Novascience@earthlink.net
         www.novapublishers.com

Printed in the United States of America

CONTENTS

PREFACE

Education is a perennially vexing issue in American life. What, exactly, is the best system for teaching? Proponents of charter schools believe that competition is the key; public schools will improve if they have to compete for students. Charters themselves are public schools, but ones run by any group accepting the challenge of improving student performance in return for fewer regulations and tight budget restrictions. In short, charter schools have defined focus and clear accountability. Those opposing the charter movement, though, claim that charter schools are divisive and distract attention from public school needs. Some politicians have shown approval of charter schools, as evidenced by President George W. Bush's bill for funding charter programs. This book aims to clear up some of the questions around charter schools and can help answer the questions surrounding the future of the American education system.

OVERVIEW OF STATE
CHARTER SCHOOL LAWS

Kimberly D. Jones

ALASKA

The State of Alaska currently permits the creation of not more than 30 charter schools in geographically diverse areas throughout the state.[1] The local school board may create its application procedure for charter schools with the input of parents, teachers, and school employees. The application should include information such as the mission of the school, a description of its administrative structure, and financial plan. Charters may be approved by the state board of education or the state board for charter schools. If approved the application becomes a contract between the school and the local school board. To that end, the application must detail the proposed educational program, expected achievement levels, administrative policies, budget, student-teacher ratio, and the proposed location of the facility.[2] To become effective, the charter application must be approved by both the local and state boards of education. Alaska charter schools are exempt from the local school districts' textbook, program, and curriculum requirements.[3] However, the schools must comply with federal, state, and local laws concerning health, safety, and civil rights. Alaska charter schools are funded

---

[1] Alaska Stat. § 14.03.250 (Michie 1996).
[2] Alaska Stat. § 14.03.255.
[3] Alaska Stat. § 14.03.255.

at the same level as a comparable non-charter public school.[4] A contract for a charter school may not exceed five years and may not be extended beyond July 1, 2005.[5]

ARIZONA

The state of Arizona established a State Board of Charter Schools consisting of the state superintendent of public instruction, three members of the general public who meet specific requirements, two members of the business community appointed by the governor, and three advisory members from the state legislature chosen by the leaders of both the state House and Senate.[6] Among the duties of the Board are selection and supervision of charter schools. Applicants seeking to establish a charter school must submit a detailed plan describing among other things, the charter school's mission, organizational structure, financial plan, and grades served.[7] Charter schools may be sponsored and the sponsor "may contract with a public body, private person or private organization for the purpose of establishing a charter school pursuant to this article."[8] Applicants are required to submit to a federal and state criminal background check.[9] Charters are granted for 15 years at which time the charter school may seek renewal. The sponsor of the charter school may deny the request for a renewal if the charter school has not met the sponsor's expectation or is not in compliance with the school's charter.

ARKANSAS

Applicants for a charter school in Arkansas must petition the State Board of Education.[10] An existing school may petition for a charter if: (1) the local school board approves; (2) the organization representing the majority

---

[4] Alaska Stat. § 14.03.260.

[5] Alaska Stat. § 14.03.275.

[6] Ariz. Rev. Stat. Ann. § 15.182 (West Supp. 1996).

[7] Ariz. Rev. Stat. Ann. § 15.183.

[8] Ariz. Rev. Stat. Ann. § 15.183(B). A sponsor may be a school district governing board, the state board of education or the state board for charter schools. Sponsors are not liable for debts or financial obligations of the charter school and most sponsors are immune from personal liability for acts taken in good faith. Id. at 15.183(P) & (Q).

[9] Id.

[10] Ark. Code Ann. § 6-10-116 (Michie Supp. 1995).

of teachers approves; (3) two-thirds of certified employees approve; and (4) if the majority of parents approve.[11] If the local school board rejects a charter school petition a copy of the board's reason for rejection are forwarded to the state board.[12] The state board may not approve a charter unless it has also been approved by the local board. Charters are approved for an initial 3-year period and may be renewed for one-year or multi-year periods not to exceed 3 years.[13]

CALIFORNIA

California limits the number of charter schools to no more than 100 operating in any school year.[14] Applicants must submit a detailed plan for the charter school including, among other things, what type of educational program will be used, measurable pupil outcomes and how those outcomes will be measured, qualifications and criminal background of employees, and the school's organizational plan.[15] An applicant for a charter school must obtain the signatures of at least 10% of teachers in the school district or 50% of the teachers at one school in the district. The petition must then be submitted to the governing board of the school district that must hold a hearing regarding the petition. While the school district cannot force students to attend charter schools,[16] a school district may petition to convert all of its schools into charter schools.[17] A petition for conversion must contain at least 50% of the signatures of teachers in the school district and meet the requirements required for submission of a charter school petition. The school district must also arrange an alternative public school for students in the district who do not want to attend the charter school. A charter, if granted, may not exceed 4 years at which point the school may seek a renewal, not to exceed 5 years. A charter may be terminated if it is found that the school violated a material part of the charter petition, failed to meet the pupil outcomes identified in the petition, or is fiscally mismanaged.[18]

---

[11] Ark. Code Ann. § 6-10-116(c).
[12] Ark. Code Ann. § 6-10-116.
[13] Ark. Code Ann. § 6-10-116(g).
[14] Cal. Educ. Code § 47602 (West Supp. 1997).
[15] Cal. Educ. Code § 47605(b)(1)-(5). "Pupil outcomes...means the extent to which all pupils of the school demonstrate that they have attained the skills, knowledge, and attitudes specified as goals in the school's educational program."
[16] Cal. Educ. Code § 47605(f).
[17] Cal. Educ. Code § 47606.
[18] Cal. Educ. Code § 47607.

COLORADO

The local board of education evaluates and approves applications for charter schools.[19] The board must hold hearings and must act on an application within 60 days.[20] An applicant for a charter school must include, among other things, the goals of the school, evidence that a charter school is supported by parents, teachers or pupils, how pupil performance will be evaluated and how the school will be governed.[21] Colorado also restricts the number of charter schools to be created and specifies that a certain number of those schools must serve at-risk pupils.[22] Charters or renewal of a charter may not exceed a time period of 5 years. A charter school seeking a renewal must submit a financial statement and a report on the progress of the school and its pupils.

CONNECTICUT

The Connecticut State Board of Education reviews and grants charters for both local and state charter schools.[23] Between July 1, 1997 and June 30, 1999, the State Board may grant no more than 12 local charter schools and no more than 12 state charter schools. An applicant for a charter school in Connecticut should contain, among other things, a detailed description of the goals, educational program and methodology of the school, the interest of the community, it financial plan and organizational structure, and qualifications of the school personnel.[24] The local school board reviews the application and holds hearings to determine the community interest within 60 days of receipt of the application. Upon approval the application is sent to the State Board of Education who must vote on the application within 75 days of receipt. A charter may be granted for a period not to exceed 5 years, at which time the charter may seek a renewal. Applications for state charter school are similar. The state board of education evaluates the charter application and holds hearings in the district where the state charter school is

---

[19] Colo. Rev. Stat. Ann. § 22-30.5-101 *et seq.* (West 1995).
[20] If the board rejects the charter school petition, the applicant may appeal to the state board of education. Colo. Rev. Stat. Ann. § 22-30.5-107(3).
[21] Colo. Rev. Stat. Ann. § 22-30.5-106.
[22] Colo. Rev. Stat. Ann. § 22-30.5-109.
[23] Conn. Gen. Stat. Ann. § 10-66bb (West. Supp. 1997).
[24] Conn. Gen. Stat. Ann. § 10-6bb(d).

to be located. The state board must vote within 75 days of receipt of the proposal.

DELAWARE

Delaware's Charter School Act of 1995 allows interested groups to submit proposals for establishment of charter schools.[25] An application for a charter school must be submitted to a local or state school board on or before December 31, if the school plans to operate during the next school year.[26] If an existing school wishes to convert to a charter school they must apply by October 30 to begin the charter school the next school year. Upon receipt of the proposal the school board must conduct hearings within 20 days. The school board must vote on the application within 90 days. Delaware lists a series of criteria to be reviewed in considering and approving a charter.[27] Some of the criteria include the charter's educational goals, evidence of community support, a plan to evaluate student progress and the financial organization of the school. If approved, the approving authority is responsible for oversight of the school and must conduct an evaluation 3 years after the school begins operation.[28] If the evaluation is unsatisfactory the charter school may be put on probationary status pending improvement.[29] If the charter is revoked or placed on probationary status, the applicant may seek arbitration by contacting the American Arbitration Association with both parties splitting the arbitration fees equally.[30]

DISTRICT OF COLUMBIA

The District of Columbia Charter Schools Act of 1996 gives the D.C. Board of Education the authority to evaluate and grant charter applications.[31] Under D.C. law, an eligible applicant includes "a person, group, or organization, including a private, public, or quasi-public entity, that is nonprofit, non-religious, nonsectarian, and non-home-based, or an institution

---

[25] Del. Code Ann. Educ. § 501-516 Supp. 1996).
[26] Del. Code Ann. Educ. § 511.
[27] Del. Code Ann. Educ. § 512.
[28] Del. Code Ann. Educ. § 515. (Oversight & Revocation Process)
[29] Del. Code Ann. Educ. § 516.
[30] Del. Code Ann. Educ. § 515(h).
[31] D.C. Code Ann. § 31.2801-31.2853 (Supp. 1997).

of higher learning that seeks to establish a public charter school or to renew a charter pursuant to this chapter."[32] After an application is submitted, the D.C. School's Superintendent will review the application to ensure it is complete, and if not, inform the applicant of any deficiency and provide reasonable assistance to the applicant.[33] Once the superintendent deems the application complete (in any case no longer than 60 days after submission), it is forwarded to the Board of Education and a hearing is held within 30 days of receipt of the application by the Board. The Board must either accept or reject the charter application within 30 days of the hearing. If the application is denied, the Board must describe its reasoning in writing and inform the applicant of the appeal's process. An applicant may appeal a denial to the Council of the District of Columbia whose decision shall be final and not subject to judicial review.[34]

Typical of most charter school applications, D.C. requires applicants to detail their instructional goals and methods, methods of student evaluation, school operational structure and budget, and the policies of the school.[35] The Board of Education will give preference to applications that address at-risk students and those that seek to locate in existing public school facilities.[36] An existing public school may apply to convert into a charter school if a majority of parents, students and faculty agree in the form of a petition. If granted, initial charter terms and renewals are for 5-year periods.[37] A Board of Trustees elected pursuant to procedures established in the charter application and consisting of faculty and parents govern the charter school.[38] Charter schools receive the same amount of funding as a comparable non-charter public school.[39] While the charter school may focus on certain grade levels or academic subject areas, it may not base admission solely on intellectual or athletic ability.[40] Current public school teachers may seek a 2-year unpaid leave of absence to teach in a charter school.[41] Employees of charter schools are not considered employees of the District of Columbia

---

[32] D.C. Code Ann. § 31.2801(2).
[33] D.C. Code Ann. § 31.2813. The Superintendent may charge a $150 application fee and may charge an administrative fee to cover the costs of administering and monitoring the charter school. However, the fee must not exceed one-half of one percent of the school's annual operating budget. D.C. Code Ann § 31.2820.
[34] D.C. Code Ann. § 31-2811.
[35] D.C. Code Ann. § 31-2812.
[36] D.C. Code Ann. § 31-2811.
[37] D.C. Code Ann. § 31-2811.
[38] D.C. Code Ann. § 31-2816.
[39] D.C. Code Ann. § 31-2823.
[40] D.C. Code Ann. § 31-2817.
[41] D.C. Code Ann. § 31-2818.

school system or government.[42] The charter school must submit an annual report to the Superintendent detailing student performance, graduation rates and test scores, the level of parental involvement and a financial statement.[43] The Board of Education may revoke or refuse to renew a charter if it finds that the school is financially unstable, not meeting the terms of its charter, or failing to make satisfactory academic progress.[44]

FLORIDA

The State of Florida allows for the formation of charter schools through creation of a new school or by conversion of a currently existing public school.[45] An application for a charter school may be submitted by an individual, teachers, parents, a group of individuals, or a legal entity organized under the laws of the State of Florida. Regarding a currently existing public school, an application for conversion may be made by the principal, teachers, parents, and/or the school advisory council at the school. At least half of the school's teachers and parents must support conversion to a charter school. A charter application should describe, among other things, the school's mission, curriculum, instructional methods, and achievement goals.

The district school board may accept, review, and sponsor a charter school in the county in which it has jurisdiction. A decision to grant an application for a charter school is made by the district school board no later than 60 days after receipt of the application. If the application is rejected, the applicant may appeal to the state board of education. Once the state board decides on the application, the state board makes a recommendation that the district school board accepts or rejects the application consistent with the state board's decision. Charters are granted or renewed in 3-year increments. A charter will not be renewed if the school (1) fails to fulfill the

---

[42] D.C. Code Ann. § 31-2818.

[43] D.C. Code Ann. § 31-2815.

[44] D.C. Code Ann. § 31-2820. Before revoking or failing to renew a charter, the Board of Education must send notice of such action to the charter school's board of trustees. The charter school may request, in writing, a hearing regarding the proposed revocation. The Board must render a detailed decision in writing after the hearing if it votes to revoke the charter. The charter school may appeal to the D.C. City Council whose decision is final and not subject to judicial review.

[45] Fla. Stat. Ann. § 228.056 (West Supp. 1998).

requirements of the charter, (2) fails to meet standards of fiscal management, (3) violates the law, or (4) for good cause.[46]

GEORGIA

The State of Georgia defines a charter as "an academic and or vocational performance based contract between the state board, a local board of education, and a local school..."[47] Charters are granted for 5-year periods and are exempt from state and local rules, regulations, policies and procedures.[48] Requests for a charter school are first approved by the local school board and then forwarded to the state board. If the local board rejects the charter application then the reasons for the rejection are forwarded to the state board. After the initial five-year period, the board may extent the charter for periods not exceeding five years. The charter proposal must include a detailed plan on how the school will meet state and national education goals. A charter may be revoked if the faculty and parents request revocation based on the failure of the school to fulfill the terms of the charter.

HAWAII

Hawaii's "student-centered schools" allow for "implementation of alternative frameworks with regard to curriculum; facilities management; instructional approach; length of the school day, week, or year; and personnel management; and may include any two or more schools acting jointly."[49] Student-centered schools are exempt from most state laws except for those laws concerning state procurement, collective bargaining, discrimination and health and safety standards. A local school board is established with consists of persons representing principals, instructional staff, support staff, parents, student body representatives and a community-at-large representative. Each representative is chosen by the corresponding group of the school. The principal is usually the chief operating officer of the school and, along with the board, is responsible for the maintenance of the

---

[46] Fla. Stat. Ann. § 228.056(10).
[47] Ga. Code Ann. § 20-2-255-256 (1997).
[48] Id.
[49] Haw. Rev. Stat. Ann. § 302A-1123 (Michie Supp. 1997).

academic standards and financial management of the school. The educational goals of the school must correspond to Hawaii's statewide educational performance standards. Charter schools must conduct annual self-evaluations and the department of education will review the school 4 years after its initial start-up. The board of education, based on a two-thirds vote, may discontinue the student-centered school if it fails to meet educational standards.

IDAHO

The Idaho legislature recently passed the Public Charter Schools Act of 1998.[50] The Act limits the number of charter schools to no more than 60 during the first 5 years of enactment. No more than 12 charter schools may be approved within one year. A charter school may be created as a new school or by converting an existing public school. However, an entire school district may not convert to charter schools. Private, parochial and for-profit entities are prohibited from becoming a charter school. Requests for a charter should be submitted to the board of trustees of a school district. An already existing public school seeking to convert to a charter must submit a petition signed by at least 60% of teachers and parents of the petitioning school. A petition for a new charter school must be signed by at least 30 "qualified electors" of the district. The board of trustees must hold a public hearing before deciding on a petition. A decision of the board of trustees may be appealed to the state superintendent of public instruction.

The charter application should define the school's educational curriculum, standards, testing methods, the school's administrative structure, qualifications of employees, and admissions procedures. Charter schools are required to submit annual reports regarding student progress and fiscal operations. Charter schools are funded similarly as other public schools. An initial charter and subsequent renewals may be granted for a period not to exceed 5 years. A charter may be revoked if it is found that the charter school has committed a material violation of the charter, failed to meet student educational standards, or for fiscal mismanagement. If the charter is revoked, an appeal may be made to the state board of education.

---

[50] Public Charter School Act of 1998, 1998 Idaho Laws Ch. 92 (H.B. 517)(West 1998).

ILLINOIS

The Illinois Charter School Law allows for no more than 45 charter schools.[51] Illinois charter schools are exempt from most state laws except those concerning background checks of school employees, tort liability, state student discipline code, abused and neglected children reporting requirements, and the Illinois School Student Records Act.[52] A proposal for a charter school should include a description of the school's educational program, how the success of the program will be measured and how the school will be governed.[53] Preference is given to a proposal that sets high academic standards, addresses at-risk students and represents "a high level of local pupil, parental, community, business and school personnel support."[54] Charters are granted for between 3-5 years and are renewed in increments not to exceed five school years. Charters may be revoked or not renewed if the school fails to fulfill the requirements of the charter, or the charter school is fiscally mismanaged or the school is in violation of applicable law. Illinois sets minimum requirements for instructional charter school personnel.[55]

KANSAS

Kansas's Charter School law limits the number of charter schools to fifteen.[56] Similarly, Kansas requires a detailed application for a charter school. The application must address the school's educational program, level of interest of the community, parents, students and teachers, program goals and how they will be measured, governance structure, qualifications of faculty and staff, health and safety standards, criteria for admission, student disciplinary policy, and the school's budget.[57] Upon submission of a charter application, the local board of education will conduct hearings. If approved, the state board of education will be notified and will approve the charter pending an evaluation of whether the charter is in compliance with applicable state and federal laws and regulations. An applicant may seek a waiver of local and state requirements that will be granted if the board of

[51] 105 Ill. Comp. Stat. Ann. § 5/27A-4 (West Supp. 1998).
[52] 105 Ill. Comp. Stat. Ann. § 5/27A-5.
[53] 105 Ill. Comp. Stat. Ann. § 5/27A-7.
[54] 105 Ill. Comp. Stat. Ann. § 5/27A-8.
[55] 105 Ill. Comp. Stat. Ann. § 5/27A-10.
[56] Kan. Stat. Ann. § 72-1904-10 (1996).
[57] Kan. Stat. Ann. § 72-1906.

education finds the reasons for the waiver "meritorious and legitimately related to successful operation of the charter school."[58] The state board of education makes the final decision of whether the waiver will be granted. The charter will be approved for an initial 3 years, after which time the charter will be reviewed for renewal or revocation. If the board of education opts not to renew or revoke the charter, a hearing must be held addressing the reasons for revocation or non-renewal.[59]

LOUISIANA

The Louisiana Charter School Demonstration Programs Law establishes four types of charter schools.[60] Type 1 is a new school established pursuant to a charter between a nonprofit corporation and a local school board. Admission to a Type 1 charter school is limited to students who would be eligible to attend a public school operated by the local school board within the same city or parish. A Type 2 charter school is a new school established pursuant to a charter between a nonprofit corporation and the State Board of Elementary and Secondary Education. Admission to a Type 2 charter school is available to students residing in the state. Type 3 is a preexisting public school converted to a charter established between a nonprofit corporation and the local school board. A Type 3 charter requires the approval of faculty and parents of the preexisting school. Admission to a Type 3 school is limited to students who would be eligible to attend a public school operated by the local school board within the same city or parish. Type 4 is a preexisting public school converted to a charter school pursuant to a charter between a local school board and the State Board of Elementary and Secondary Education. The requirements and admission criteria for a Type 4 charter school are the same for a Type 3 charter school.

The State Board of Education and Secondary Education and the local school boards must review proposed charter applications in a timely manner and render a decision after holding a public hearing. Applicants for a charter school must come from one of six groups: teachers, citizens, public service organizations, business or corporate entities, a Louisiana college or university or the faculty or staff of any city or parish public school or any local school board.[61] Applications for Types 1, 2, and 3 charter schools must

---

[58] Kan. Stat. Ann. § 72-1906.
[59] Kan. Stat. Ann. § 72-1907.
[60] La. Rev. Stat. Ann. § 17:3971-4001 (West Supp. 1998).
[61] La. Rev. Stat. Ann. § 17:3983.

be submitted to the local school board that has jurisdiction where the school is to be located. If the local school board rejects a charter application, the applicant may submit a proposal for a Type 2 charter school to the State Board of Elementary and Secondary Education. The State Board must notify the local school board upon receipt of a Type 2 proposal and must allow the local school board and other interested groups to provide written information regarding the proposal and to appear at a public hearing prior to a final decision of the State Board. A proposal for a Type 3 charter school may only be submitted to a local school board and a rejection by the local school board terminates the Type 3 application process. The local school board must notify the State Board of charters entered into by the local school board. After May 31, 2001 only a local school board may enter into a charter if the total number of charter schools allowed by the law has not been exceeded. The law allows for a possible maximum of 42 charter schools.

Louisiana requires that 75% of the instructional staff at a charter school be certified teachers, while the remaining 25% must meet minimum state requirements.[62] Private schools, parochial schools and home-based schools are prohibited from becoming charter schools. A charter will be granted for 5 years, but will be evaluated after the third year. They may be renewed for additional 5-year periods. According to Louisiana law, "[N]o charter shall be renewed unless the charter renewal applicant can demonstrate, using standardized test scores, improvement in the academic performance of students over the term of the charter school's existence."[63] Charter schools are exempt from most state and local school regulations, except health and safety requirements, minimum requirements for graduation from public schools, open meetings and public records, school attendance, required courses of study, religious liberty of students, and sex education, among others.[64] Charter schools must adhere to state and federal laws concerning "civil rights and individuals with disabilities."[65]

MASSACHUSETTS

Massachusetts provides for two types of charter schools, commonwealth charter schools and Horace Mann charter schools. Commonwealth charter schools are typically those schools newly created by a charter. Horace Mann

---

[62] La. Rev. Stat. Ann. § 17:3991.
[63] La. Rev. Stat. Ann. § 17:3992.
[64] La. Rev. Stat. Ann. § 17:3996.
[65] La. Rev. Stat. Ann. § 17:3996.

charter schools are currently existing public schools that have converted to charter school status or a charter school within a public school. Applications for charter schools must be submitted to the board of education each year by November 15. The board must review applications and render decisions by February of the next year.[66] The board of education may grant charters for 5-year periods. If the charter is approved, the school is managed by a board of trustees which is independent of any school committee. The board of trustees is responsible for establishing the school's curriculum and annual budget. Private and parochial schools are prohibited from applying for a charter, but businesses, teachers and parents are encouraged to apply. Colleges, universities and museums are also encouraged to seek charters. Only 50 charters may be granted under Massachusetts's law. Out of that 50, 37 must be commonwealth charter schools while the remaining 13 are reserved for Horace Mann charter schools.[67] Preference for admission to a charter school is given to students residing in the school district where the school is located and to applicants whose siblings are already at the school. Massachusetts charter schools "operate in accordance with its charter and the provisions of law regulating other public schools."[68] Charter school students are "required to meet the same performance standards, testing and portfolio requirements set by the board of education for students in other public schools."[69] Public school teachers wishing to teach in a charter school will be granted a two-year leave of absence. An additional two-year extension may be granted and at the end of four years the teacher has the option of returning to the old assignment or resigning to continue teaching in the charter school. Probationary status may be given to a failing charter school to allow for a remedial plan. If the remedial plan fails or if the charter school is otherwise not fulfilling its charter, the charter may be revoked.

A Horace Mann charter school is a charter operated by the local school committee and the local collective bargaining agent in which the school is located.[70] Charters for Horace Mann schools are granted by the board of education and the schools operate independently of the school committees that approve them. The charter application for both types of charter schools are the same, except Horace Mann charter applications must describe the non-instructional services that will continue to be provided by the local school district. A preference in admission to Horace Mann charter schools

---

[66] Mass. Gen. Laws Ann. ch. 71, § 89 (West Supp. 1998).
[67] If less than thirteen applications are received for Horace Mann charter schools within three years of the statute, then the limit of Horace Mann charter schools is reduced to five.
[68] Mass. Gen. Laws Ann. ch. 71, § 89(h).
[69] Mass. Gen. Laws Ann. ch. 71, § 89(h).
[70] Massachusetts Charter Schools Amendments, ch. 46, S.B. 1849 (July 11, 1997).

will be given to students actually enrolled in the school on the date the application for a charter is filed, then to their siblings, then students actually enrolled in the public schools of the district where the Horace Mann charter school is located, and finally to other resident students. Horace Mann charter schools are exempt from local collective bargaining agreements but employees remain members of the collective bargaining unit and accrue benefits entitled to them under the collective bargaining agreement.

MICHIGAN

Michigan's "Public School Academies" are public schools operating as a corporate body and governmental agency.[71] An "authorizing body" consisting of a school board, community college or state university may seek to enter into a contract for a public school academy with the state board. The authorizing body's responsibilities include selecting and setting the terms of the public academies' board of directors. The authorizing body receives the state school aid payment that they are responsible for distributing to the public school academy.[72] The state board must submit annual comprehensive reports on public school academies which describe the school's mission statement, attendance statistics, dropout rate, test scores and financial stability.[73] An application for a public school academy should include, among other things: (1) articles of incorporation; (2) purpose of the academy; (3) copy of proposed bylaws for the academy; (4) description of governance structure and (5) description of school's educational goals, curricula and pupil assessment.[74] The authorizing body is responsible for oversight of the academy unless the state board of education finds that the authorizing body is not properly evaluating the academy. An authorizing body may not charge a fee or seek reimbursement of expenses for considering an application for a contract or oversight for an "amount that exceeds a combined total of 3% of the total state school aid received by the public school academy in the school year in which the fees or expenses are charged."[75] A proposal may be presented to the local school board. If the proposal is rejected, the applicant may petition the board to "place the question of issuing the contract on the ballot to be decided by the school

---

[71] Mich. Comp. Laws Ann. § 380-501-517a (West Supp. 1998).
[72] Mich. Comp. Laws Ann. § 380.507.
[73] Mich. Comp. Laws Ann. § 380.501a.
[74] Mich. Comp. Laws Ann. § 380.502.
[75] Mich. Comp. Laws Ann. § 380.502(6).

electors of the school district."[76] Teachers in public school academies must be certified unless the academy is operated by a state university of community college and the teacher is a full-time tenured or tenure-track professor of the institution. In addition to meeting the requirement listed above, an academy operated by a community college can employ non-certified teachers if the teacher has 5 years of teaching experience in the subject.[77]

Michigan also allows for "chartered educational clinics". "A chartered educational clinic is a specialty public school academy and shall only serve public school pupils...during hours outside the pupil's normal class hours by providing special assistance for up to 3 hours per week, pursuant to a written prescription by the principal of the public school in which the pupil is regularly enrolled on recommendation of a teacher of the pupil."[78] The requirements for chartered educational clinics are the same the same for public school academies. The contract for both public school academies and chartered educational clinics may be revoked for failure to fulfill terms of the charter, violation of the law or failure to meet general public sector accounting principles. A decision to revoke by the authorizing body is not subject to administrative or judicial review.[79]

MINNESOTA

The goals of Minnesota's "results-oriented charter schools" are to "improve pupil learning; increase learning opportunities for pupils; encourage the use of different and innovative teaching methods; require the measurement of learning outcomes and create different and innovative forms of measuring outcomes; establish new forms of accountability for schools; or create new professional opportunities for teachers, including the opportunity to be responsible for the learning program at the school site."[80] To this end, Minnesota allows for the authorization of no more than 40 charter schools in the state.[81] To apply for a charter school application, a sponsor[82] may seek

---

[76] Mich. Comp. Laws Ann. § 380.503.
[77] Mich. Comp. Laws Ann. § 380.505.
[78] Mich. Comp. Laws Ann. § 380.505a.
[79] Mich. Comp. Laws Ann. § 380.507.
[80] Minn. Stat. Ann. § 120.064 (West Supp. 1998).
[81] A currently operating public school may convert to a charter school upon approval by at least ninety percent of the school's full-time teachers.
[82] A sponsor is defined as, "A school board, community college, state university, technical college, or the University of Minnesota." Minn. Stat. Ann. § 120.064 subd. 3.

approval from the local school board. The sponsor must submit a written contract listing how the charter school plans to meet the goals outlined by the state.[83] If the local school board refuses to sponsor a charter school the applicant may appeal to the state board of education.[84]

A charter school is operated by an elected board of directors chosen by staff members and parents. Licensed teachers of the school must constitute a majority of the school's board of directors. Similar to most charter schools, Minnesota's charter school law explicitly states that the charter schools are nonsectarian public schools and are prohibited from charging tuition.[85] While exempt from most state laws and regulations, Minnesota charter schools must still satisfy health and safety standards. The charter school must submit annual reports to its sponsor and the state board of education.[86] Charter school contracts "may be up to three years."[87] A sponsor may opt not to renew for "failure to meet the requirements for pupil performance contained in the contract; failure to meet generally accepted standards of fiscal management; for violations of law; or other good chase shown."[88]

MISSISSIPPI

The State of Mississippi recently enacted a Charter Schools Pilot Program.[89] Mississippi's charter schools program is limited to currently existing public schools. The Pilot Program is limited to six local schools throughout the state. A local school may submit an application requesting charter school status after such application is approved by the local school board, a majority of school faculty, and a majority of the parents of enrolled students. The application must also describe how the school plans to improve student learning and meet state education goals and how the school plans to measure such progress.

After a school sends a petition for a charter to the local school board, the school board will consider the request and then forward it to the state board of education. If a petition is rejected by the school board, the state board of

---

[83] Minn. Stat. Ann. § 120.064 subd. 5.
[84] An applicant may only appeal to the state board of education if at least two members of the local school board vote in favor of the charter application. If approved, the state board sponsors the charter school. Minn. Stat. Ann. § 120.064 subd. 4.
[85] Minn. Stat. Ann. § 120.064 subd. 8.
[86] Minn. Stat. Ann. § 120.064 subd. 14.
[87] Minn. Stat. Ann. § 120.064 subd. 5.
[88] Minn. Stat. Ann. § 120.064 subd. 21.
[89] Miss. Code Ann. § 37-28-1 (West Supp. 1997).

education may request a hearing to gather further information. The state board of education grants charters for a 4-year term and such charters may be renewed on a one-year or multi-year basis not to exceed four years. A charter school may receive funding from public and private sources. A charter may be terminated if a majority of the faculty and parents make such a request to the state board of education. The state board of education may nullify the charter if it finds that the school is not meeting the terms of the charter. The state board of education must submit annual reports regarding the status and progress of charter schools in the state. The Mississippi Charter Schools Pilot Program contains a sunset provision that the program will end after July 1, 2001.

NEVADA

The State of Nevada recently enacted legislation creating charter schools.[90] A board of trustees of a school district must apply to the state department of education to sponsor charter schools within the school district. Once the state board of education accepts the board of trustees' application, the trustees shall provide public notice of its ability to sponsor charter schools and solicit charter school applications. Applicants for a charter school should include three licensed teachers. These licensed teachers may apply for a charter alone or with ten or more members of the general public, representatives of an organization devoted to service to the general public, representatives of a private business, or representatives of certain state colleges and universities. This group of applicants is referred to in the Nevada statute as a "committee." A committee seeking a charter must submit an application to the department of education. The charter application must describe what educational programs will be offered by the charter school, what educational services will be offered to at-risk students, the admissions policy, the standard of achievement and how that achievement will be measured. Applicants must agree to provide a written report to parents, the school's community, and the state education officials at the end of each school semester. While a charter school is exempt from most state education regulations, Nevada does require that 75% of charter schoolteachers be licensed.

---

[90] Nev. Rev. Stat. Ann. § 386.500.610 (Michie Supp. 1997).

NEW HAMPSHIRE

New Hampshire offers two educational alternatives, open enrollment public schools and charter schools.[91] An open enrollment school is defined as "any public school which, in addition to providing educational services to pupils residing within its attendance area or district, chooses to accept pupils from other attendance areas within its district and from outside its district."[92] A charter school is defined as "an open enrollment public school, operated independent of any school board and managed by a board of trustees."[93] Charter schools operate as nonprofit secular organizations under a charter granted by the state board. Before a school district may consider a charter school open enrollment contract, it must adopt the provisions of state law establishing charter schools during its annual meeting. If the school district does not conduct annual meetings, the legislative body of the school district must seek a petition from a percentage of registered voters, hold hearings, and place the issue on the ballot during a regular election.[94]

New Hampshire exempts its charter schools from state and local rules that are applicable to non-charter public schools, while providing charter schools with the same rights and privileges as non-charter public schools. Charter schools are governed by a board of trustees which must apply to the local school board for a charter before July 1 of the year before the school is scheduled to open. Eligible trustees include nonprofit organizations, a group of two or more state certified teachers, or a group of ten or more parents.[95] Currently existing public schools may apply to convert to a charter school if they obtain school board approval, a percentage of teachers approve such a conversion, and the school superintendent and principal agrees to the conversion in writing.[96] The board of trustees' application should be in the form of a contract addressing elements required by the state. There are twenty-four elements ranging from the school's proposed curriculum to proposals for encouraging parental involvement.[97] The school board evaluates and decides to either approve or reject the prospective board of trustees' contract. The board's decision is then forwarded to the state board that will also evaluate the prospective trustees' contract. If the state board

---

[91] N.H. Rev. Stat. Ann. § 194-B:1-22 (West Supp. 1997).
[92] N.H. Rev. Stat. Ann. § 194-B:1(VI).
[93] N.H. Rev. Stat. Ann. § 194-B:1 (III).
[94] N.H. Rev. Stat. Ann. § 194-B:5.
[95] N.H. Rev. Stat. Ann. § 194-B:3(V). See also N.J. Rev. Stat. Ann. § 194-B:5 describing the duties and responsibilities of the board of trustees.
[96] N.H. Rev. Stat. Ann. § 194-B:3(VI).
[97] N.H. Rev. Stat. Ann. § 194-B:3.

approves the contract, it will issue a charter. If approved by the state board the contract is sent to the school district for a vote by the school district's legislative body that may ratify the contract submitted by the trustees or reject it. The decision of the school district's legislative body is final. Charters are granted for 5-year terms, but the state provides for termination, renewal, or amendment of a charter. Renewal terms are for 7 years. An applicant seeking to amend its charter contract must submit a written amendment to the school board that has thirty days to approve or reject the amendment. If the amendment is rejected, the school may appeal to the state board that also has thirty days to evaluate and issue a decision. If the state board approves the amendment, the local school board must execute it; but final approval or rejection rests with the school district legislature.[98]

NEW JERSEY

New Jersey's Charter School Program Act of 1995 allows for the creation of 135 charter schools within a four-year period, with a minimum of three charter schools per county.[99] Charters are granted for an initial four-year period and then may be renewed for a 5-year period. New Jersey also limits the number of students in a newly created charter school to no more than 500 students or 25% of the district's student body, whichever is less.[100] Parents, teachers, institutions of higher education, and private entities may submit an application for a charter school.[101] Currently existing public schools may convert to a charter school if 51% of the school's teachers and 51% of the school's parents sign a petition requesting conversion to a charter school. A board of trustees manages the school on behalf of the sponsors and the school district subject to the school's charter. Charter school applications must be submitted to the commissioner and the local board of education or to the state superintendent, if the school district is state operated. The commissioner of the school board has final authority to accept or reject a charter application. However, the local board of education may appeal to the state board of education. Information required in the charter school application does not differ substantially from what is required in other states. However, some distinctions do exist. Significantly, New Jersey charter schools are not automatically exempt from state and local regulations, but

---

[98] N.H. Rev. Stat. Ann. § 194-B:3(XI).
[99] N.J. Stat. Ann. § 18A:36A-1-18 (West Supp. 1997).
[100] N.J. Stat. Ann. § 18A:36A-4.
[101] N.J. Stat. Ann. § 18A:36A-4.

they must describe and justify in their application any waiver from state or local regulations they seek.[102] However, teachers are required to be certified by the state.

Public schools converting to charter schools are subject to the applicable bargaining agreement. Newly created charter school employees are subject to the collective bargaining agreement only if the board of trustees agrees pursuant to the school's charter. Public school teachers may seek a three-year leave of absence from the local school board or state superintendent to pursue work in a charter school. If a charter is granted, the commissioner conducts annual assessments of the school to ensure compliance with its charter and the commissioner's findings are used in determining if a charter should be renewed. The commissioner may revoke a charter if the school fails to satisfy the charter's terms. A charter school may be placed on probationary status pending the outcome of remedial efforts to gain compliance with the charter. If remedial efforts fail, the commissioner has authority to revoke the charter.

NEW MEXICO

New Mexico enacted its charter school legislation with the hope that it would "encourage the use of different and innovative teaching methods."[103] The act allows for the authorization of five charter schools. Charters are granted for periods not exceeding 5 years and may be renewed at 5-year intervals. Applicants apply through their local school board to the state board of education. The local school board is encouraged, but not required, to evaluate and make a recommendation regarding the charter application. The state board may authorize a charter school if the applicant submits an application showing that at least 65% of the school's teachers signed a petition in support of becoming a charter school, parents support the charter proposal, and present a detailed operational plan and budget.[104] New Mexico does not automatically exempt its charter schools from state and local regulations but does allow them to seek waivers.

---

[102] See N.J. Stat. Ann. N.J. Stat. Ann. § 18A:36A-10 describing the facility that a charter school may be located in and how such facilities are exempt from most facility regulations, except those concerning health or safety. See also N.J. Stat. Ann. § 18A:36A-11 which allows the commissioner to grant waivers to state and local regulations, except those concerning "assessment, testing, civil rights and student health and safety."

[103] N.M. Stat. Ann. § 22-8A-1-7 (West Supp. 1997).

NORTH CAROLINA

North Carolina's charter school program has at least six goals: (1) improve student learning; (2) increase learning opportunities for at-risk students; (3) encourage innovative teaching methods; (4) create new opportunities for teachers; (5) expand educational choices available to parents; and (6) hold schools accountable through measurable results of student outcomes.[105] North Carolina limits itself to 100 charter schools statewide with no more than five charter schools per year in one local school district. Charters are granted for 5-year periods and are renewable for periods not to exceed 5 years. A board of directors governs the operation of the school. Eligible applicants include any person, group of persons, or non-profit corporation.[106] Existing public schools may convert to a charter school if the majority of teachers and parents support conversion. An application may be submitted to either the local board of education, the state board of education, or to the University of North Carolina. The state board of education has final authority to accept or reject a charter school application. Charter schools are bound to follow applicable health and safety standards, minimum academic standards, and civil rights laws.[107] A percentage of charter schoolteachers must be certified. A teacher in an already existing public school who wishes to teach in a charter school must be granted a leave of absence for an unlimited duration. A charter may be terminated or not renewed for violation of the charter, applicable laws, or at the request of the school's faculty.[108]

OHIO

In the State of Ohio, charter schools are referred to as "Community Schools." A community school is defined as "a public school, independent of any school district, and is part of the state's program of education."[109] A community school may be sponsored by a city, local, exempted village, or joint vocational board of education of the school district where the school is

[104] N.M. Stat. Ann. § 22-8A-5.
[105] N.C. Gen. Stat. § 115C-238.29A-29G (Michie Supp. 1997).
[106] N.C. Gen. Stat. § 115C-238.29B(a).
[107] N.C. Gen. Stat. § 115C-238.29F.
[108] N.C. Gen. Stat. § 115C-238.29G.
[109] Ohio Rev. Cole Ann. § 3314.01 et seq. (Anderson Supp. 1997).

to be located, or by the state board of education. An existing public school may convert to a community school. A proposal to create a new school as a community school may be submitted by a big eight school district. A "big eight school district" is defined as a school district that for fiscal year 1997 had a percentage of children residing in the district and participating in Ohio Works First greater than thirty percent and had an average daily membership greater than 12,000.[110] In the case of a new school in a big eight district, the sponsor may be the board of education of the big eight district, the board of education of any joint vocational school district, the board of education of any other city, local, or exempted village school district, or the state board of education. A proposal for a contract for a community school should describe a comprehensive program detailing the school's academic goals, education program, fiscal management, and qualifications of teachers, among other things. An initial contract for a community school may not exceed 3 years.

OREGON

While Oregon does not have legislation specifically addressing charter schools, charter schools do exist. The legislature and the Governor or Oregon support the creation of charter schools through Oregon's Alternative Education Program law.[111] An "alternative education program" is defined as a "school or separate class group designed to assist students to achieve the goals of the curriculum in a manner consistent with their learning styles and needs."[112] The Oregon Legislature enacted legislation that would expand the Alternative Education Programs law to cover the creation of charter schools.[113] Shortly thereafter, the Governor of Oregon issued an Executive Order directing the State Board of Education to issue regulations regarding the formation of charter schools under the Alternative Education Programs law.[114]

---

[110] Id.

[111] Or. Rev. Stat. § 329-860 (1996).

[112] Or. Rev. Stat. § 336.615 (1996).

[113] Oregon Alternative Education Programs, Ch. 164 (S.B. 184)(May 20, 1997).

[114] Steven Carter, Kitzhaber Order Seeks to Boost Charter Schools, Portland Oregonian, Aug. 7, 1997, at B01.

PENNSYLVANIA

The Pennsylvania Charter School Law seeks "to provide opportunities for teachers, parents, pupils and community members to establish and maintain schools that operate independently from the existing school district structure..."[115] A charter school may be established by individuals, teachers, parents, colleges or universities, corporations or an association. A charter school may be a newly created school or a public school wishing to convert to a charter school.[116] To convert a currently existing public school to a charter school, an applicant must show by way of a written petition that at least fifty percent of faculty and parents support a charter school. A charter school application should describe the involvement of teachers, parents, and the community and the educational program of the charter school.

To start a new school, an application must be submitted to the local board of school directors. The local board of school directors must hold at least one public hearing within 45 days of receiving the charter application. The local board must allow for at least 45 days after the first public hearing before rendering a decision on the application.[117] In any case, a final decision must be rendered not later than 75 days after the first public hearing.[118] A charter may be approved for a period of no less than 3 years and no more than 5 years. Charters may be renewed for 5-year periods.

If an application is denied, the local board of school directors should notify the applicant in writing clearly describing the deficiencies in the application. A denied application may be revised and resubmitted. In addition, a denied application may be appealed to the Charter School Appeal Board, which was established under the Pennsylvania Charter Schools Law.[119] To appeal an application denied by the local board of directors, the applicant must obtain signatures of at least 2% of the residents, 18 or older,

---

[115] 24 Pa. Cons. Stat. Ann. § 17-1725-A (West Supp. 1998).

[116] Section 1718-A establishes the option of Regional Charter Schools. A Regional Charter School may be established by the boards of school directors of one or more school districts.

[117] An exception of thirty days is made for charter schools beginning during the 1997-1998 school year. Pennsylvania Charter Schools Law, S.B. 123, Section 1717-A(b)(3)(d).

[118] Again, the statute makes a provision limiting the time to 60 days for charter schools beginning during the 1997-1998 school year.

[119] Section 1721-A establishes the State Charter School Appeal Board. The Board consists of seven members, one of which is the state secretary of education. The other members are appointed by the governor with the consent of a majority of the Senate. The board members must include a parent of a school-aged child, school board member, active certified teacher, school faculty member or administrator, member of the business community and a member of the state board of education.

in the school district or one thousand residents, whichever is less, within 60 days of the denial. The appeal board must act on the application within 60 days of receipt. A denial of a charter by the appeal board is reviewable by the Commonwealth Court.

A charter may be revoked or not renewed if the local board of school directors finds that the charter school has violated a material term of the charter, failed to meet student performance requirements, failed to meet fiscal management requirements or any violation of applicable laws. Notice of revocation or non-renewal should be given to the governing board of the charter school. The local board of school directors must hold a hearing and render a final decision within 30 days of the hearing. The charter school may appeal to the State Charter School Appeal Board. A decision by the Appeal Board is reviewable by the Commonwealth Court.

PUERTO RICO

Puerto Rico provides for Special School Districts that are used "for the purposes of testing pedagogical innovations..."[120] The Secretary of Education is authorized to establish the Special School Districts and the necessary rules and procedures for maintaining them.

RHODE ISLAND

The Charter Public School Act of Rhode Island allows for a maximum of twenty charters by July 1, 1997.[121] Eligible applicants for a charter school are public school personnel, public school districts and existing public schools.[122] Applicants must apply to either the commissioner of elementary and secondary education or the school committee in the district where the school would be located. An existing public school may convert to a charter school if a majority of parents support the conversion and two-thirds of certified teaching personnel approve the charter. A charter school proposal should include, among other things, a description of "a plan for education, including the mission, objective, method of providing a basic education, and process for improving student learning and fulfilling the charter, and

---

[120] P.R. Laws Ann. tit. 18, § 1901-1904.
[121] R.I. Gen. Laws § 16-77-11 (1997).
[122] R.I. Gen. Laws § 16-77-3.

fulfilling state and national educational goals and standards.[123] Charter schools are bound by most state laws and regulations.[124] Charters are granted for a 5-year period subject to 5-year renewal periods. Proposals for a newly created charter school must show that one-half of parents and at least two-thirds of certified teaching personnel would support the charter school. Once an eligible group has submitted a complete application, the commissioner or board conducts a public comment period and holds at least two public hearings.[125] The commissioner or school board will either accept or reject the charter school application within ninety (90) days after the conclusion of the public comment period. Rhode Island charter schools are funded at the same level as non-charter public schools. Other services provided to school districts such as transportation, food services and maintenance may be contracted between the school district and the charter school and paid for out of charter school revenue. Complaints regarding the performance of a charter school may be made to the charter school's governing body, and if not adequately addressed, then to the commissioner.

SOUTH CAROLINA

South Carolina is one of the latest states to enact charter school legislation. The South Carolina Charter Schools Act of 1996 was enacted to allow additional educational opportunities for students and parents, as well as, greater professional development for teachers.[126] Applications for charter schools must be submitted to the local school board of trustees of the school district where the charter school would be located.[127] Potential applicants must elect a charter committee that will submit an application and organize the charter school as a non-profit corporation.[128] The charter application constitutes a contract between the charter school and its sponsor. The sponsor may be either the local board of education or the state board of education, depending on which approves the charter application.[129] Once

---

[123] R.I. Gen. Laws § 16-77-4.

[124] R.I. Gen. Laws § 16-77-11.

[125] R.I. Gen. Laws § 16-77-5.

[126] S.C. Code Ann. § 59-40-10 - 59-40-190 (Law Co-op. 1996).

[127] S.C. Code Ann. § 59-40-60.

[128] The local school district must provide technical assistance to those interested in establishing a charter school. S.C. Code Ann. § 59-40-140(H). The state board of education is responsible for providing information regarding charter schools and the application process to interested applicants. S.C. Code Ann. § 59-40-150.

[129] S.C. Code Ann. § 59-40-70(E).

approved the application becomes a contract between the governing board of the charter school and the local school district. An existing public school may convert to a charter school if both two-thirds of the school's faculty and parents agree to the conversion.[130] The approval and renewal period of the charter school is 3 years.[131] A progress report of the charter school must be submitted along with the renewal application.[132]

The local school board, before granting or denying a charter school application, must hold community meetings. The board must issue a decision within 90 days of receiving the application.[133] If an application is denied, a written explanation for the denial must be forwarded to the state board of education. The applicant has the option of addressing the reasons for denial and re-submitting the application or appealing to the stated board of education.[134] Upon receipt of an appeal, failure to renew or revocation of a charter, the state board of education must hold a public hearing. If the state board disagrees with the local board's decision, it must remand the application back to the local board with its findings and instructions.[135] Upon remand, the local school board has thirty days to conduct a public hearing and reconsider its decision, which becomes final. A final decision of the local school board or of the state board of education is subject to judicial review in the circuit court for the county where the applicant sought to locate the charter school.[136]

An employee of the local school district may seek a leave of absence for up to 5 years to teach in a charter school.[137] However this provision does not apply to employees of a converted public school.[138] Charter schools receive the same amount of state and federal funding as a comparable non-charter

---

[130] S.C. Code Ann. § 59-40-100(A). The principal submits the application on behalf of the school. In terms of employee benefits and compensation, teachers and other employees of the converted charter school remain employees of the local school district. The converted charter school must reimburse the local school district for employer contributions paid on behalf of these teachers and employees. S.C. Code Ann. § 59-40-100(C).

[131] S.C. Code Ann. § 59-40-110(A).

[132] S.C. Code Ann. § 59-40-110(B).

[133] S.C. Code Ann. § 59-40-70. If a decision is not rendered within ninety days, the charter is considered approved.

[134] S.C. Code Ann. § 59-40-70(D).

[135] S.C. Code Ann. § 59-40-90(C)(1).

[136] S.C. Code Ann. § 59-40-90(C)(2).

[137] S.C. Code Ann. § 59-40-130(A). Upon termination of the leave of absence, a teacher may return to his former employee status but is not guaranteed a return to the same school. An employee on leave under this provision continues to accrue employee benefits under the South Carolina Retirement System.

[138] S.C. Code Ann. § 59-40-130(C).

public school would receive.[139] Charter schools must submit annual reports to the local school district and the state department of education detailing its progress in meeting the goals of its charter. The state board of education must evaluate and publish its findings on existing state charter schools.[140]

A charter may be revoked if it is found that the school has violated the terms of the charter, failed to meet the goals of the charter contract, is mismanaged or violated any applicable laws.[141] The governing body of the charter school must receive 60 days notice of any adverse action and be given the opportunity to hold a hearing to address the concerns of the sponsor.[142] Any action regarding the charter school is abated upon conclusion of the hearing and its appealable to the state board of education.[143]

South Carolina charter schools are exempt from state and local regulations that govern public schools, but they may choose to comply with such regulations. However, charter schools are required to meet health and safety requirements, minimum attendance requirements, financial management, and civil rights laws, among others.[144]

TEXAS

The State of Texas allows for the creation of no more than twenty charter schools.[145] Those eligible to apply for a charter include an institution of higher education, non-profit organization, or a governmental entity.[146] Charter schools are subject to state, federal and local regulations governing public schools.[147] The state board of education is responsible for creating and implementing the application process and criteria for charter school applicants according to requirements of state law.[148] At a minimum, a charter

---

[139] S.C. Code Ann. § 59-40-140. The charter school must contract with the local school district for services such as: custodial, food, maintenance, curriculum and media services, libraries and warehousing.

[140] S.C. Code Ann. § 59-40-160.

[141] S.C. Code Ann. § 59-40-110.

[142] S.C. Code Ann. § 59-40-110(E). Any assets or property belonging to the charter school upon dissolution reverts back to the local board of education.

[143] S.C. Code Ann. § 59-40-110(F).

[144] S.C. Code Ann. § 59-40-50.

[145] Tex. Educ. Code Ann. § 12.101-118 (West 1998).

[146] Tex. Educ. Code Ann. § 12.101.

[147] Tex. Educ. Code Ann. § 12.103-104.

[148] Tex. Educ. Code Ann. § 12.110. The board may gauge parental support by either requiring a petition in support of a charter school or through a public hearing. The board's criteria must require information regarding improvement of student performance and the financial

application should include, among other things, a description of the educational program offered, a minimum level of student performance, grade levels to be served, school's organizational structure, and the qualifications of the teachers.[149] If approved, the charter becomes a contract between the state board of education and the chief operating officer of the charter school.[150] Charter schools are evaluated annually.[151]

Teachers in charter schools are eligible to participate, or in the case of a conversion, to continue to participate in the state's requirement plan.[152] Charter schools receive the same level of funding as a comparable non-charter school.[153] A charter may be revised, revoked or terminated if the state board of education finds that the school has violated the terms of the charter, the school is fiscally mismanaged or otherwise violates any applicable law.[154] The state board of education is responsible for establishing a procedure for revising, revoking or terminating a school's charter that must include a right to a hearing.[155]

UTAH

The Utah legislature recently enacted the "Schools for the 21 Century Program."[156] The Act creates a variety of educational reforms and includes the "Utah Charter Schools Act." It creates a 3-year pilot program that allows for the creation of 8 charter schools. A charter school may be created by opening a new school or converting an existing public school. Potential applicants include individuals, groups, teachers, parents, and non-profit entities. To convert an existing school into a charter, a petition must be filed that is signed by two-thirds of the school's parents and teachers. The initial proposal must be submitted and approved by the local school board with final approval by the state board of education. Parochial and home schools are prohibited from becoming charter schools. The charter application should

---

impact the charter school would have on existing schools in the district. Also see Tex. Educ. Code Ann. § 12.111 for the required content of a charter school application.
[149] Tex. Educ. Code Ann. § 12.111.
[150] Tex. Educ. Code Ann. § 12.112.
[151] Tex. Educ. Code Ann. § 12.118.
[152] Tex. Educ. Code Ann. § 12.105. Both the school district and the state retain the responsibility to make any contributions to the retirement plan that they would have to make if the teacher was an employee of a non-charter school.
[153] Tex. Educ. Code Ann. § 12.107.
[154] Tex. Educ. Code Ann. § 12.115.
[155] Tex. Educ. Code Ann. § 12.116.
[156] Schools for the 21st Century Program, 1998 Utah Law Ch. 231 (H.B. 145)(West 1998).

include information such as the age and grade level to be served, administrative structure, financial plan, methods of assessing students, and qualifications of teachers. The charter school is required to make annual progress reports to the state and local boards of education and the state legislature. The charter school is exempt form most regulations and laws except those concerning health, safety, and civil rights. The state provides funding for the charter school, including start-up costs and transportation.

VIRGINIA

Virginia's new charter school bill defines a charter school as "a public, nonsectarian, non-religious, or non-home-based alternative school located within a public school division."[157] A charter school may be created as a new school or an existing public school may be converted into a charter school. A charter application may be submitted by any person, group, or organization. The approved application shall serve as a contract between the sponsors of the charter school and the local school board. The application should include, among other things, a mission statement, educational goals, evidence of community support, statement of need, how students will be assessed, and a financial plan. Most rules and regulations do not apply to charter schools, except those concerning civil rights. The local school board must conduct public hearings regarding a charter school application and the decision made by the local school board is final and not subject to appeal. The number of charter schools shall not exceed 10% of the school district's total number of schools. A charter application or renewal may not be granted for a term beyond 3 years.

WISCONSIN

Applicants wishing to open a charter school must first file a petition signed by either 10% of teachers in the school district or at least 50% of the teachers at one school in the district.[158] In addition to the signatures, the petition should include, among other things, the name of the person applying

---

[157] Establishment of Charter Schools, 1998 Virginia Laws Ch. 890 (S.B. 318)(West 1998).
[158] Wis. Stat. Ann. § 118.40 (West Supp. 1997). According to § 118.40(2m), the school board may contract with an individual or group to operate a charter school. However, the school board is bound by the same requirements as any other applicant applying for a charter.

for the charter, description of the educational program, the organizational structure of the school, minimum educational goals and the methods the school will use to measure and achieve them, qualifications of the teachers, and public school alternatives for students who do not wish to attend or cannot attend the charter school.[159] Upon receiving the petition, the school board must hold a hearing within 30 days where the board will consider the level of employee and parental support for the charter school.[160] All public schools in a district may be converted to charter schools if at least 50% of the teachers in the district sign a petition and alternative public school arrangements are made for students not wishing to attend a charter school.[161] Within 30 days of the public hearing the school board must either accept or reject the petition for a charter school.[162] If the petition is approved, it creates a contract between the person named in the petition and the school board. The terms of the contract are the provisions of the petition and any others agreed to between the parties. In any case, a charter term (including renewal terms) may not exceed 5 years.[163] An applicant may file an appeal within thirty days of the denial to the state department of education. The department then has 30 days to make a decision regarding the denial and the department's decision is final.[164]

Funding for the charter school is specified in the provisions of the petition. Charter schools are subject to certain restrictions. Namely, charter schools cannot charge tuition, they must be non-sectarian, and must not discriminate on the basis of race, sex, religion, disability, etc. The school board may refuse to renew or revoke a charter if the board finds that the terms of the charter have been violated, the school is fiscally mismanaged, students are failing to make progress, or the school has violated an applicable law.[165]

---

[159] Wis. Stat. Ann. § 118.40(1m)(b).
[160] Wis. Stat. Ann. § 118.40(2).
[161] Wis. Stat. Ann. § 118.40(2)(b). Charter schools must give preference to pupils who reside in the attendance area of the school, if the schools replace a public school in whole or in part. Wis. Stat. Ann. § 118.40(4).
[162] Wis. Stat. Ann. § 118.40(2)(c).
[163] Wis. Stat. Ann. § 118.40(3)(b).
[164] Wis. Stat. Ann. § 118.40(2)(c).
[165] Wis. Stat. Ann. § 118.40(5).

WYOMING

Applicants wishing to open a charter school must file a petition with the district board of trustees.[166] The petition must contain the signatures of at least 10% of teachers and parents in the district or in the alternative 50% of both teachers and parents of one school in the district.[167] Within thirty days of receiving the petition, the district board must hold a public hearing and the board must render its decision within 60 days of receiving the petition.[168] Charters may be granted or renewed for periods not exceeding 5 years.[169] The petition should include, among other things, a description of the school's educational program, the methods the school will use to measure and improve pupil outcomes, the organizational structure of the school, qualifications of the teachers, admission requirements and alternative public school arrangements for students who do not want to attend or are not admitted to the charter school.[170] Wyoming law requires that full-time teachers in charter schools be certified by the state.[171] Regarding admission policies, a charter school cannot charge tuition, must give preference to a student residing in the attendance area of a converted public school, and must not rely solely on academic ability for admission.[172] A charter may be revoked if the charter school violates the terms of the charter, is fiscally mismanaged or violates any applicable law.[173] The district board of trustees should evaluate annually the performance of the charter schools in the state.

---

[166] Wyo. Stat. Ann. § 21-3-201 (Michie 1997).
[167] Wyo. Stat. Ann. § 21-3-203.
[168] Wyo. Stat. Ann. § 21-3-203.
[169] Wyo. Stat. Ann. § 21-3-204.
[170] Wyo. Stat. Ann. § 21-3-203.
[171] Wyo. Stat. Ann. § 21-3-203.
[172] Wyo. Stat. Ann. § 21-3-203(d).
[173] Wyo. Stat. Ann. § 21-3-204.

PUBLIC CHARTER SCHOOLS: STATE DEVELOPMENTS AND FEDERAL POLICY OPTIONS

Wayne Riddle and James Stedman

INTRODUCTION[1]

Charter schools are a relatively new type of public school that is released from many of the forms of regulation that normally apply to public school in return for increased accountability in terms of outcomes for pupils. Approximately two-thirds of the states have enacted legislation authorizing the establishment of charter schools in recent years, and over 1,600 charter schools are currently operating, although approximately 55% of the schools are located in only four states (Arizona, California, Michigan, and Texas). State charter school laws and policies vary widely, especially with respect to the degree of autonomy provided to the schools. In some states, individual charter schools are treated as if they were independent local educational agencies (LEAs), or school districts, that receive funding directly from the state and are not subject to the authority of the traditional LEA serving their locality.

A federal Public Charter Schools program helps to support the establishment of charter schools in the states where they are authorized.

---

[1] Note: The original version of this report was also prepared, in part, by Steven Aleman, a former Specialist in Social Legislation.

While moderate in size, funding for this program has grown rapidly since it was first authorized in 1994. On October 22, 1998, the President signed into law H.R. 2616, the "Charter School Expansion Act of 1998" (P.L. 105-278). This legislation revised the Public Charter Schools statute in several respects, primarily to increase and extend its authorization; give priority for grants to states that provide charter schools with financial autonomy, have increased their number of charter schools, provide means by which charter applicants may appeal decisions not to grant a charter, and periodically review the performance of such schools; and to expand technical assistance to charter schools, especially regarding their eligibility for federal aid programs.

Concerns have been expressed by some education policymakers and analysts about possible barriers to equitable participation by charter schools in the full range of federal education assistance programs, particularly in the schools' first year of operation. This is especially an issue in states where charter schools are treated as separate LEAs because requirements such as minimum grant size thresholds or reporting and other administrative responsibilities may limit participation by charter school LEAs.

This report provides an overview and analysis of charter school legislation and related activity in the states, the federal Public Charter School program, and issues that have arisen regarding the participation of charter schools in other federal education assistance programs. More specifically, this report provides:

- A general description of charter schools;
- A discussion and analysis of the major characteristics of state charter school laws, especially in three states that we surveyed in detail (Arizona, California, and Minnesota);
- A review of the federal Public Charter Schools program;
- A description of the provisions of P.L. 105-278, the "Charter School Expansion Act of 1998;"
- An analysis of the treatment of charter schools under major federal education assistance programs;
- A discussion of general issues regarding charter schools, such as start-up problems, accountability, facilities requirements, and the role of charter schools in school reform efforts; and
- Federal policy options regarding the Public Charter Schools program.

DEFINITION AND DESCRIPTION
OF CHARTER SCHOOLS

Charter schools are public schools established under state law, they do not charge tuition; and they are nonsectarian. These schools enter into charters with authorized chartering entities and are granted varying degrees of autonomy from state and local rules and regulations. In exchange for this autonomy, they are held accountable for meeting the terms of their charters, including achievement of academic and related outcomes stipulated in the charters.

There is wide variation among the states in the terms and conditions under which charter schools can be established and operated. **Depending upon the particular state law,** these schools may be newly created or established from existing public or private schools; they may be established by private or public organizations, teachers, parents, or other private citizens.[2] Students are not mandatorily assigned to these schools; rather, they choose these schools and are admitted if they meet admissions requirements, if any, and if space is available for them. Available data suggest that many of the charter schools established to date are relatively small.[3] In comparison to other public schools, charter schools are less likely to be elementary schools, and are more likely to serve students at a wide range of grade levels (e.g., grades 6 or 7-12, K-8, or even K-12). As of the 1997-1998 school year, approximately 70% of charter schools were newly-created schools, while almost 20% were converted from pre-existing public schools and 11% were converted from pre-existing private schools.[4]

---

[2] For a recent comparison of state charter school laws, see *A Comparison of Charter School Legislation*, prepared under contract to the U.S. Department of Education by RPP International. December 1998. 64 p.

[3] A series of annual reports published by the U.S. Department of Education – (*A Study of Charter Schools: First Year Report*, by RPP International and the University of Minnesota, 1997 (Hereafter cited as **ED**, *A Study of Charter Schools: First Year Report*), followed by *A National Study of Charter Schools: Second Year Report* released in August 1998 (Hereafter cited as **ED**, *A National Study of Charter Schools: Second Year Report*), and *The State of Charter Schools: Third Year Report*, released in May 1999 (Hereafter cited as **ED**, *A National Study of Charter Schools: Third Year Report*)) – indicate that the median enrollment for charter schools in 1997-1998 was 132 students, compared to a median enrollment of 486 students for all public schools in the states with charter schools in operation.

[4] ED, *A Study of Charter Schools: Third Year Report.*

STATE LAWS[5]

Thirty-six states plus the District of Columbia and Puerto Rico have thus far adopted legislation that authorizes the establishment of charter schools.[6] This legislation has been adopted over a relatively brief time period – Minnesota was the first state to authorize charter schools, in 1991. The number of charter schools actually in operation currently also varies widely among the states. Reportedly, as of September 1999, there were 1,682 charter schools in operation nationwide. Twenty-one states and the District of Columbia are reported as having 10 or more charter schools in operation in September 1999 – Alaska (18), Arizona (348), California (234), Colorado (68), Connecticut (17), District of Columbia (28), Florida (112), Georgia (32), Illinois (19), Kansas (15), Louisiana (17), Massachusetts (39), Michigan (175), Minnesota (57), Missouri (14), New Jersey (52), North Carolina (83), Ohio (48), Pennsylvania (45), South Carolina (10), Texas (168) and Wisconsin (45). Five states with charter school laws thus far have no such schools in operation. Fifty-five percent of all current charter schools are in just four states – Arizona, California, Michigan, and Texas.[7]

State charter school laws are often compared and contrasted with respect to a number of specific characteristics, several of which are noted below. More broadly, many analysts characterize charter school laws as providing "more" or "less" autonomy or freedom from regulation by state and local educational agencies. These two groups of state laws are not completely distinct – e.g., not all of the states categorized as providing "more" or "less" autonomy share every specific characteristic typically associated with these groups, and some state laws have characteristics associated with both

---

[5] See also CRS Report 97-769, *Overview of State Charter School Laws*, by Kimberly D. Jones.
[6] The states (and the year in which charter school legislation was adopted) are: Alaska (1995); Arizona (1994); Arkansas (1995); California (1992); Colorado (1993); Connecticut (1996); Delaware (1995); District of Columbia (1996); Florida (1996); Georgia (1993); Hawaii (1994); Idaho (1998); Illinois (1996); Kansas (1994); Louisiana (1995); Massachusetts (1993); Michigan (1993); Minnesota (1991); Mississippi (1997); Missouri (1998); Nevada (1997); New Hampshire (1995); New Jersey (1996); New Mexico (1993); New York (1998); North Carolina (1996); Ohio (1997); Oklahoma (1999); Oregon (1999); Pennsylvania (1997); Rhode Island (1995); South Carolina (1996); Texas (1995); Utah (1998); Virginia (1998); Wisconsin (1993); and Wyoming (1995). **Source:** The Center for Education Reform, Charter School *Highlights and Statistics* (Hereafter cited as Center for Education Reform, *Charter School Highlights and Statistics*). Downloaded November 9, 1999 from the Internet [http://www.edreform.com/pubs/chglance.htm].
[7] Center for Education Reform, *Charter School Highlights and Statistics*.

categories. Nevertheless, state charter school laws are generally characterized[8] as providing **"more" autonomy** if the laws:

- set either very high, or no, limits on the number of charters that may be granted;
- set few or no limits on what sorts of individuals or groups may apply for a charter;
- allow charters to be granted not only for conversion of existing public schools but also for totally new schools and/or existing schools that previously were private;
- authorized a wide variety of entities to grant charters (e.g., state education board(s), colleges and universities, local education agencies, etc.);
- treat individual charter schools as if they were separate LEAs, and provide for the allocation of state, federal, and perhaps certain local, revenues directly to the charter schools, without "regular" LEAs being involved;
- provide financial and technical assistance for acquisition (purchase or leasing) of school facilities, meeting other school startup costs, and/or meeting the administrative responsibilities of participating in federal or state aid programs;
- specify that charter schools are entitled to receive federal, state, and perhaps local, revenues per pupil that are not less than those allocated to "regular" LEAs;
- waive a wide variety of state regulations, particularly with respect to labor-management relations (such as collective bargaining with teacher and other employee organizations), while releasing the schools completely (or almost so) from control or regulation by "regular" LEAs;
- do not require teachers or other staff to meet certification requirements that apply to such staff in "regular" LEAs and schools;
- provide relatively long-term charters that do not have to be renewed frequently (e.g., 5 years or longer); and

---

[8] See, for example, Center for Education Reform, *Charter School Highlights and Statistics*. Also, see Finn, Chester E., *et al. Charter Schools in Action: What Have We Learned?*, the Hudson Institute. 1996. (Hereafter cited as Finn, Charter Schools in Action). Downloaded January 1997 from the Internet [http://www.al.com/hudson/charters].

- allow flexibility in the selection of accountability criteria to be used to determine whether a charter should be renewed.

In contrast, state charter school laws are often described as providing **"less"** **autonomy** if the laws:

- set relatively low limits on the number of charters that may be granted in any year, or in the aggregate;
- allow only limited types of individuals or groups (e.g., certified teachers) to apply for charters;
- allow charters to be granted only for conversion of existing public schools (often requiring the approval of the existing school's staff and/or parents;
- authorize only one, or a very small number, of entities to grant charters;
- treat charter schools as part of a "regular" LEA for such purposes as allocation of revenues;
- provide little or no financial or technical assistance for acquisition of facilities, other startup costs, or meeting administrative responsibilities under federal or state aid programs;
- either do not specify the level of local, state, or federal revenues that charter schools are entitled to receive, or specify that they are to receive an amount per pupil that is less than the amount received by schools in "regular" LEAs;
- waive only a limited number of state and/or local regulations, often excluding all aspects of labor-management relations from waiver, and/or require that all waivers be individually negotiated with the entity authorized to grant the charter;
- require teachers and other staff to meet certification requirements and other qualifications that apply to public school staff statewide;
- limit charters to a relatively brief time period (e.g., 2-3 years); and
- allow little or no flexibility in the selection of accountability criteria which will be the basis for determining whether charters should be renewed.

The second- and third-year reports of ED's *A Study of Charter Schools* found that two trends appear to be emerging among states that are revising charter school legislation adopted earlier. The study found that these states are generally increasing, or even eliminating, previous limits on the maximum number of charter schools that may be established, and that they are frequently providing increased flexibility in the procedures by which charters are granted (for example, increasing the number of entities authorized to grant charters, offering avenues for appeal of disapproval of charter petitions, or making it easier to establish eligibility to apply for a charter).

Thus far, there seems to be a correlation between the degree of autonomy provided by a state's charter school law and the number of schools that are established. For example, most of the states with large numbers of charter schools have been identified by several analysts as having charter legislation that provides "more" autonomy. This may seem quite unsurprising, given that one of the criteria distinguishing "more" from "less" autonomous is the limit on the number of schools that may be established. However, in many states offering "less" autonomy to charter schools, the number of schools established thus far is well below any limit that has been set. Thus, the variance in number of schools among states seems to result more from difference in incentives to establish schools, or barriers to establishing schools other than explicit numerical limits.

Specific State Laws

We provide more specific information on the charter school laws of three states – Arizona, California, and Minnesota. These states were selected because they are among those with the largest number of charter schools in operation and/or the longest-existing charter school laws, and because they exemplify a varied range of charter school policies.[9]

Arizona

In Arizona, charters to operate schools may be granted by the State Board of Education, a State Board of Charter Schools, or "regular" LEAs. Schools chartered by one of the two state boards have more autonomy than

---

[9] Information in these summaries comes from a variety of sources, including telephone conversations with state education agency staff.

those chartered by a "regular" LEA. The state-chartered schools are generally treated as separate LEAs, and receive state and federal revenues directly via the state educational agency (SEA). In contrast, schools chartered by "regular" LEAs have less autonomy, and are generally treated as being part of that "regular" LEA, even if they are not located within the geographical boundary of that LEA (as is sometimes the case).

Arizona places no limits on the number of charters that may be granted by "regular" LEAs; a limit of 25 per year is placed on the number of charters that may be granted by each of the two state boards. A distinctive characteristic of the Arizona legislation is that charters may be granted for a period of up to 15 years without renewal. Reportedly, this relatively long time period for charters was adopted to make it easier for charter schools to make long-term commitments to lease or purchase facilities. With such a lengthy time period before charters must be renewed, it may be difficult to enforce charter school accountability requirements, although charters are to be "reviewed" every 5 years.

The number of charter schools in Arizona has grown rapidly since charters were first authorized in 1994. There were no charter schools until the 1995-1996 school year, when 46 schools began operations. In 1996-1997, there were a total of 164 charter schools, 96 chartered by a state board and the remainder by "regular" LEAs, and in September 1999 there were reportedly 348 total charter schools in Arizona. A very wide variety of groups and schools may receive a charter, including new schools and formerly private schools (as long as they were not religiously-affiliated schools). Arizona is often characterized as being the state where it is easiest to receive a charter and begin school operations, as well as being a state where charter schools are highly autonomous, at least if chartered by a state entity. Charter schools in Arizona are granted a "blanket" waiver of a wide range of state regulations that apply to other public schools. Teachers in Arizona charter schools need not be certified, and the schools need not engage in collective bargaining with teacher organizations.

California

The original California charter school law, adopted in 1992, was substantially revised in May 1998, and this discussion is based on the amended legislation, which took effect beginning in the 1998-1999 school year. In California, charter schools are generally established by the "regular" LEA within whose geographic boundaries the proposed charter school would be located. However, refusal by a LEA to grant a charter may be appealed to either the County or State Board of Education, in which case either of these boards may grant the charter and accept responsibility for overseeing the charter school. Traditional public schools may be converted into charter schools only if 50% of the teachers at a school to be converted into a charter school "sign off" of the application. However, petitions to establish a wholly new charter school (i.e., not the conversion of an existing public school) may be submitted by 50% of the parents of prospective pupils at the school or 50% of the prospective teachers at the school. Formerly private schools may not be converted into public charter schools. Charter schools may, at their option, operate as non-profit ("public benefit") corporations.

Beginning in the 1999-2000 school year, the revised California charter school law provides that "...charter school operational funding shall be equal to the total funding that would be available to a similar school district serving a similar pupil population..."[10] Charter schools are generally treated as part of the "regular" LEA in which the school is located, although they may choose to receive state and federal program revenues either via the "regular" LEA or directly.

The original statute authorizing charter schools in California limited their total number to 100 schools statewide, although this cap had been exceeded with no more than 10 in a single LEA. However, the statewide cap has been raised to a total of 250 charter schools in 1998-1999, with an additional 100 schools allowed each year thereafter,[11] and the cap of 10 charter schools per LEA (22 for Los Angeles) has been eliminated. As of September 1999, there were 234 charter schools operating in California. Some of the charter schools are independent study or home school programs connected through computer networks – i.e., not conventional "school facilities" at all. Charter schools in California are granted a "blanket" waiver of a wide range of state regulations that apply to other public schools. Charters are granted for a period of 5 years. Teachers in California charter schools must be certified, and legislation adopted in 1999 provides collective bargaining rights to charter schoolteachers, if they should seek them, although bargaining may be separate from that for the "regular" LEA. Charter schools must meet all statewide performance standards and conduct all pupil tests required of other public schools in the state.

---

[10] Section 47613.5 of the California Code. Note that "operational funding" is defined to exclude capital funds for facilities. Regulations to implement this provision have not yet been drafted.

[11] These limits may be waived by the State Board of Education.

With the adoption of the May 1998 legislative amendments, charter schools in California have been granted substantially increased autonomy, although still not so much as under the Arizona charter school law.

Minnesota

Minnesota adopted the nation's first charter school law in 1991. The authorized number of charter schools was originally "capped" under the Minnesota law; the initial cap was eight schools, which was later raised to 40 schools. Currently, there is no cap on the number of charter schools that may be approved in Minnesota. The number of operating charter schools has grown from 2 in 1992-1993 to 57 in September 1999. Many of the schools serve a largely disadvantaged student population.

Schools must apply for a charter to a "regular" LEA (not necessarily the one for the area in which the school would be located) or a variety of public and private institutions of post-secondary education in the state. Refusals to approve charter applications may be appealed to the state board of education in some cases. Charters are granted for a period of up to 3 years; charter schools must report data on pupil participation and outcomes annually.

All charter schools are treated as separate LEAs in Minnesota. The statute authorizing establishment of charter schools provides generally that these schools should receive state and federal program funds directly. The schools receive no local funds. The funding provided by the state to charter schools is approximately equal to the state average revenue per pupil for general purposes.

Amendments to Minnesota's charter school legislation that were adopted in July 1997 include provision of start-up grants and facilities leasing funds, in addition to elimination of the cap on the number of charter schools. One-time start-up grants are the greater of $50,000, or $500 per enrolled pupil, for each new charter, in addition to funds that may be available under the federal Public Charter Schools program. Annual lease grants to charters may be up to $1,500 per enrolled pupil. Charter schools are also eligible for state categorical funds, as well as relevant federal grants.

Formerly private schools may become public charter schools in Minnesota. Local collective bargaining agreements for teachers and other unionized staff do no apply when charter schools are established, although a charter school's teachers may form and receive recognition of their own bargaining unit afterward. Teachers at a charter school must be certified, and a majority of a charter school's board must consist of teachers at the school.

An existing public school may be converted into a charter school only if at least 60% of the school's teachers support the conversion.

FEDERAL LAW

Public Charter Schools Program – Provisions as Amended in 1998[12]

The Public Charter Schools (PCS) program was initially authorized in 1994 in Title X, Part C of the Elementary and Secondary Education Act. It was substantially amended at the end of the 105th Congress by H.R. 2616, the "Charter School Expansion Act of 1998" (P.L. 105-278). The following discussion is based on the PCS legislation *as amended* by P.L. 105-278. It should be noted that while the rest of the Elementary and Secondary Education Act is being considered for amendment and reauthorization by the 106th Congress,[13] this activity has not thus far included the PCS program, since it was extended and amended by the 105th Congress.

The PCS program is intended to support the design, initial implementation, and evaluation of charter schools, and to stimulate expansion of the number of "high quality" charter schools. Under this authority, funds are provided, for up to 3 years, to SEAs in states with charter school laws to support a grant program for "eligible applicants" (the individuals or groups seeking to establish and administer charter schools applying in partnership with the entities authorized to grant charters) to assist them in planning their educational program (such assistance may be provided for up to 18 months), the initial implementation of their school (up to 2 years), or dissemination of information and technical assistance by

---

[12] There are two other federal education programs under which funds are explicitly authorized to be used to support charter schools. One is the Goals 2000: Educate America Act (P.L. 103-227). Under Goals 2000, SEAs are authorized to use state grant (Title III) funds reserved at the state level (not more than 10% of total state grants) for various reform activities including promoting public charter schools. Second, in addition to revising the PCS program legislation, P.L. 105-278 amended ESEA Title VI, Innovative Education Program Strategies, to explicitly authorize use of Title VI funds by both SEAs and LEAs to support planning, design, and initial implementation of charter schools. However, considering the very broad range of purposes for which ESEA Title VI finds may be used (the program is generally considered to be an elementary-secondary education block grant), it is highly likely that SEAs and LEAs were already authorized to use grants under this program to support charter schools, and this amendment will have primarily a symbolic impact.

[13] See CRS Issue Brief 98047, *Elementary and Secondary Education: Reconsideration of the Federal Role by the 106th Congress*, by Wayne Riddle, James Stedman, and Paul Irwin.

established charter schools (up to 2 years). No more than one grant may be made to a charter school for planning and initial implementation (combined), and one for dissemination/technical assistance. In addition, no more than 10% of state's PCS funds may be used for dissemination/technical assistance grants. Eligible applicants can apply directly to the U.S. Secretary of Education (ED) for funding if their state is not participating.

Grantee "Selection Criteria" and New "Priority Criteria"

In determining eligibility for, and the amount of, PCS grants for each participating state, or individual schools in states where the SEA does not participate in the program, the Secretary is to consider the following *selection criteria* with respect to *all* funds in *all* years: (1) the contribution the funds will make to helping educationally disadvantaged and other students meet state education standards; (2) the degree of flexibility provided by the state education agency (SEA) to charter schools; (3) the ambitiousness of the objectives of the state's charter school program; (4) the quality of the strategy for assessing the achievement outcomes of charter schools; (5) the likelihood that a state's grant program supported with these federal funds will meet its objectives and improve education; (6) the number of charter schools that are operating, or are approved to operate, in the state; and (7) if the state proposes to use any funds for dissemination/technical assistance grants, the quality of those proposed activities.[14]

In addition to the *selection criteria* described above, which apply to the granting of all PCS funds in all years, P.L. 105-278 establishes a series of new *priority criteria* that apply to the granting of appropriated funds *in excess of $51 million* per year for *FY1999 through FY2001*, and to *all* PCS funds beginning in *FY2002*. In making grants with these designated funds, ED is to give priority to states[15] that require review and evaluation of each charter school by the relevant charter-granting authority at least once every 5

---

[14] For LEAs that apply directly to ED for PCS funds (in states that do not participate in the program), there are also seven *selection criteria*, although these differ slightly from those for SEAs. Five of these criteria are essentially the same as (2)-(5) and (7) above. The 6th LEA grant criterion is "the quality of the proposed curriculum and instructional practices;" and the 7th is "the extent of community support for the application."

[15] It is not clear how these *priority criteria* are being applied to individual "eligible applicants" (charter schools or LEAs) that apply for PCS grants (as occurred for FY1999 in Arizona, Arkansas, Hawaii, Mississippi, Nevada, and New Hampshire). While it might be surmised that such individual charter school applicants would receive priority treatment only if they are in states where the charter school law meets the *priority criteria*, it is not yet certain that this is occurring.

years, to determine whether the school is meeting the academic performance goals established in its charter; *and* that meet *one or more* of the following priority criteria: (1) the number of "high quality" charter schools has increased in the state in the period preceding the grant application, (2) the state provides either for one or more chartering authorities in addition to traditional LEAs, or for appeal of decisions not to grant a charter by such LEAs, or (3) charter schools in the state have a "high degree" of fiscal autonomy.

Some of the priority criteria established by the 1998 amendments to the PCS legislation may be subject to substantial interpretation. For example, how will it be determined that a state provides a "high degree" of autonomy over its budgets and expenditures? How does this concept differ from treatment of charter schools as separate LEAs? How would this priority apply to states where there are different classes of charter schools, some of which have much more fiscal autonomy than others (e.g., Arizona or Massachusetts)? While ED staff have presumably begun to interpret these provisions in their determination of FY1999 PCS program awards, that were announced in August 1999, it is not fully clear how they have done so; for example, the relevant grant application notice simply repeated the statutory provisions verbatim.

Another issue that has arisen with respect to these new priority criteria is whether they are "overly prescriptive" regarding state policies. Some have complained that, although they are broad and their precise impact may be unclear, these priorities signal to states that only a relatively autonomous model of charter schools should receive federal support under the PCS program, and that this represents inappropriate federal intrusion into the evolution of state policies for these schools. They also argue that as an experiment, a wide-ranging variety of types of charter school models should be established by states, and all of these should benefit from federal aid, not just one variety that has been pre-determined to be preferable.

In response to these concerns, it might be noted that: (a) the priorities affect the awarding of only a portion of appropriations for the PCS program until FY2001; (b) most competitive/discretionary (i.e., not formula) grant programs administered by ED (a category that includes the PCS program) include numerous statutory and administrative priorities to be applied in the awarding of funds; (c) the PCS statute has always contained *selection criteria*, some of which are not very different in nature from the new *priority criteria*, to be applied in awarding grants; and (d) the PCS program remains relatively small, and states that object to the priorities may refuse to apply for assistance. Nevertheless, there are very few other ED programs that include discretionary or competitive grant award priorities that involve broad state policies affecting all schools of a certain type (not just the specific schools directly receiving federal aid under the program).

For participating SEAs and charter schools, the Public Charter Schools program provides substantial authority to the Secretary to waive federal statutory or regulatory requirements. If requested in an approved application, the Secretary is authorized to waive **any** statutory or regulatory requirement over which he or she "exercises administrative authority" (except for the definition of a "charter school" for purposes of this federal program) if such a waiver would further the purposes of the program.

SEAs are permitted to reserve up to 5% of their grants annually for administrative expenses. Up to 10% of grants may be reserved by SEAs to establish revolving loan funds, from which new charter schools may borrow to help begin operations. The Secretary of ED may reserve the greater of 5% of the program's annual appropriation or $5 million, but in no case more than $8 million, for technical assistance and information dissemination to, and evaluation of, charter schools.[16]

The 1998 amendments to the PCS legislation require both ED and participating SEAs to take necessary steps to ensure that each charter school receives the grants under other federal education programs for which the school is eligible within 5 months of the opening or expansion of the school.[17] Charter school administrators and teachers are to be consulted by ED when the Department develops regulations affecting the PCS program or charter school participation in other federal education programs. At the same time, ED and SEAs are required to attempt to minimize the paperwork burdens for charter schools of participation in federal education aid programs. Finally, SEAs and LEAs are required to ensure that pupil records, including those related to the Individuals with Disabilities Education Act (IDEA), are transferred along with pupils moving to or from charter schools and other public schools.

Charter schools can be supported under this program only if they meet specific eligibility requirements. Among these requirements are the following: the school is established under the authority of a "specific State statute authorizing the granting of charters to schools" (Section

---

[16] A $2.1 million contract was awarded in 1995 for a 4-year evaluation of charter schools.

[17] The 5-month time limit may not apply in cases where the school opens after November 1 of an academic year.

10310(1)(A));[18] the school is exempted from significant state and local rules that would limit management and operational flexibility; it is created as a public school or is converted from an existing public school;[19] it is nonsectarian in its programs, admissions, policies, and employment, and is not affiliated with a sectarian entity; it does not charge tuition; it complies with specified federal civil rights statutes;[20] it is a school to which parents choose to send their children and it uses a lottery to admit students if the number of eligible applicants exceeds available capacity; it meets all applicable federal, state, and local health and safety requirements; and it has a written performance contract that provides for measurement of pupil performance "pursuant to state assessments that are required of other schools" (Section 10310(1)(L)). In addition, guidance published by ED states that charter schools for which the charter is held by a for-profit private entity are not eligible for assistance under the PCS program.[21]

The program's annual authorization of appropriations, budget request, and appropriations for FY1995-FY2000 are provided in the table below.

---

[18] Previous adoption on P.L. 105-278, the PCS eligibility provision referred more broadly to schools established under "an enabling State statute." The change in statutory language to "a specific State statute" seems likely to affect only one state which had initially participated in the PCS program – Oregon. During FY1995-1997, Oregon received PCS funds on behalf of schools chartered under broad statutory authorization for alternative schools, not a specific charter school law. The Oregon legislature has considered, but not yet adopted, specific charter school legislation in recent years.

[19] According to ED's "non-regulatory guidance" for the PCS program, "There is no provision nor mechanism in the law for converting private schools into public charter schools" [which would be eligible for aid under this program]. However, the guidance also states that "The ESEA does not foreclose a newly-created public school from using resources previously used by a closed private school or from involving the parents and teachers who may have been involved in the closed private school." See *Public Charter Schools Program: Nonregulatory Guidance For-Profit Entities, Private School Conversions, Admissions, and Lotteries*. March 1999. 5 p. Available on the Internet at: [http://www.uscharterschools.org/res_dir/res_primary/fed_gud_pcsp.htm]. In practice, there have apparently been instances where a pre-existing private school has closed, and a newly-created public charter school, which has received assistance under the PCS program, has been established shortly thereafter in the same facility and with many of the same staff and people.

[20] Those specified are the Age Discrimination Act of 1975, Title VI of the Civil Rights Act (discrimination on basis of race, color, or national origin), Title IX of the Education Amendments of 1972 (discrimination on the basis of gender), Section 504 of the Rehabilitation Act of 1973 (discrimination on the basis of disability), and Part B of the Individuals with Disabilities Education Act.

[21] These may be distinguished from schools which are managed by a for-profit entity which is under contract to a public or private/non-profit entity, which schools may be eligible for assistance under the PCS program. See U.S. Department of Education. *Public Charter Schools Program: Nonregulatory Guidance For-Profit Entities, Private School Conversions, Admissions, and Lotteries*, March 1999. 5 p. Available on the Internet at: [http://www.uscharterschools.org/res_dir/res_primary/fed_gud_pcsp.htm].

Table 1. Funding for Public Charter
Schools Program FY1995-FY2000

Fiscal year	Authorization	Budget request	Appropriation
1995	$15,000,000	$15,000,000	$6,000,000
1996	such sums as may be necessary	$20,000,000	$18,000,000
1997	"	$40,000,000	$50,987,000
1998	"	$100,000,000	$80,000,000
1999	$100,000,000	$100,000,000	$100,000,000
2000	such sums as may be necessary	$130,000,000	$145,000,000

FY1995 grants were made to 10 states (Arizona, California, Colorado, Georgia, Louisiana, Massachusetts, Michigan, Minnesota, Oregon, and Texas), and to two schools in New Mexico. By FY1999, $95 million in grants were awarded to SEAs or individual charter schools in 32 states, the District of Columbia and Puerto Rico.[22] These consisted of $41 million in first (of three) year grants to 19 states, the District of Columbia, and Puerto Rico, and $54 million in second or third year grants to 13 states. FY1999 grants were made to SEAs in Alaska, California, Colorado, Connecticut, Delaware, District of Columbia, Florida, Georgia, Idaho, Illinois, Louisiana, Massachusetts, Michigan, Minnesota, Missouri, New Jersey, New York, North Carolina, Ohio, Oklahoma, Oregon, Pennsylvania, Puerto Rico, Rhode Island, South Carolina, Texas, Utah, Virginia, and Wisconsin; *to individual charter schools or LEAs* in Arizona, Mississippi, Nevada, and New Hampshire; and to *both* the SEA and individual charter schools or a LEA in Arkansan and Hawaii.

---

[22] U.S. Department of Education. *Clinton Announces $95 Million in Support for Charter Schools.* August 28, 1999.

Charter Schools for the District of Columbia

The FY1996 District of Columbia appropriations legislation (P.L. 104-134) authorized establishment of charter schools in the District of Columbia. These schools could be established as new schools or from existing public or private schools. Charters could be granted by the board of education, a public charter school board, or other entity that may be authorized by the city council. The public charter school board has been established, and it, along with the board of education have granted charters to a total of 28 schools in operation as of September 1999.

District of Columbia charter schools are operated as independent LEAs. They have to meet requirements similar to those described above for the federal Public Charter Schools program (e.g., non-sectarian, comply with civil rights statutes, admit students by lottery if over-subscribed). Charters can be revoked if terms of the charter are violated or there is fiscal mismanagement; one such charter has been revoked thus far.

SELECTED PROBLEMS OR ISSUES REGARDING FEDERAL PROGRAMS AND CHARTER SCHOOLS

While experience with charter schools is still relatively limited in most states, certain problems or issues have arisen in the states we surveyed or have been mentioned in available research and evaluation literature. These problems and issues are discussed below. The list below should be considered to be preliminary and by no means exhaustive. It should also be kept in mind that this report considers only education assistance programs administered by ED. Such non-ED programs as the school lunch and breakfast programs of the Department of Agriculture, or support of science education by the National Science Foundation or the Department of Energy, are not considered.

Limited data on charter school participation in federal aid programs is provided in the first year report of ED's *A National Study of Charter Schools* (p. 23-24). The authors of this report surveyed states with charter schools operating in 1995-1996 to determine how many charter schools were eligible for, and how many actually received, ESEA Title I funds. According to this survey, out of a national total of 225 responding charter schools, 137 (61%) indicated that they were eligible for ESEA Title I grants, but only 65 of these (47% of schools reported as eligible) actually received Title I funds in that year. Similar findings are reported in the second year report of ED's national study of charter schools: for the 1996-1997 school year, just over two-thirds of the surveyed charter schools (69%) reported that they were eligible for Title I grants; however, only about one-half (53%) of these reportedly eligible schools actually participated in the program. The authors of these reports provide no explanation for this low rate of participation in Title I by reportedly eligible charter schools.

In March 1999, ED published a comprehensive guidance document on participation by charter schools in the Department's assistance programs, *Accessing Federal Programs: A Guidebook for Charter School Operators and Developers.*[23] This document provides detailed "non-regulatory guidance" to charter school operators, SEAs, and staff of "regular" LEAs with which some charter schools may be associated, on charter school participation in major federal elementary and secondary education programs. Earlier, ED published guidance on the treatment of charter schools under the largest federal elementary and secondary education program, ESEA Title I. In March 1998, ED published "non-regulatory guidance" on allocation of ESEA Title funds to charter schools.[24] ED has also published guidance, in a question-and-answer format, on the application of federal civil rights laws to charter schools.[25] Finally, additional guidance has been published on specific aspects of the PCS program itself.[26]

Issues Specific to the Individuals with Disabilities Education Act (IDEA)

The Individuals with Disabilities Education Act (IDEA) authorizes 10 programs to support and improve early intervention and special education for

[23] As of November 16, 1999, this document was available on the Internet at: [http://www.uscharterschools.org/tech_asst/menu_federal.htm].

[24] U.S Department of Education. Office of Elementary and Secondary Education. *Nonregulatory Guidance: Allocations to Public Charter Schools Under Title I, Part A of the Elementary and Secondary Education Act.* On the Internet, see: [http://www.uscharterschools.org/res_dir/res_primary/fed_gud_title1.htm].

[25] U.S. Department of Education. Office for Civil Rights. *Questions and Answers on the Application of Federal Civil Rights Laws to Public Charter Schools.* On the Internet, see: [http://www.uscharterschools.org/res_dir/res_primary/ocr_q&a.htm] (August 3, 1998).

[26] U.S. Department of Education. *Public Charter Schools Program: Nonregulatory Guidance For-Profit Entities, Private School Conversions, Admissions, and Lotteries.* March 1999. 5 p. Available on the Internet at: [http://www.uscharterschools.org/res_dir/res_primary/fed_gud_pcsp.htm].

infants, toddlers, children, and youth with disabilities. The IDEA Amendments of 1997, P.L. 105-17, revised and extended these programs. P.L. 105-17 includes four new provisions specifically on charter schools, as well as other amendments generally affecting charter schools.

IDEA includes three formula grant programs, authorized in parts B and C, to assist states in serving children with disabilities in different age ranges. Further, part D of IDEA authorizes seven discretionary grant programs to support reform, research, personnel development, information dissemination, and other national activities on early intervention and special education. The centerpiece of IDEA is the grants to states program, which helps SEAs, LEAs, and other agencies to serve school-age children with disabilities. The 1997 IDEA Amendments added four new provisions specifically on charter schools:

- Charter schools that are part of a LEA and the disabled children who attend them must be treated equitably by the LEA. The LEA must serve those children with disabilities enrolled in charter schools in the same way it serves children with disabilities enrolled in other public schools. In addition, the LEA must provide IDEA funds to charter schools in the same manner as it provides IDEA funds to other public schools. Prior law did not address the treatment of non-LEA charter schools. This provision, in part, is intended to ensure that non-LEA charter schools get their "fair share" of IDEA aid.[27] (Section 613(a)(5))

- Unless explicitly authorized under the state's charter school statute, a SEA may not require charter schools that are LEAs under state charter school law to file a consolidated IDEA application with another LEA. In general, SEAs may require small LEAs to file joint applications for IDEA assistance to promote effective services. This provision is intended to preserve the autonomy of LEA charter schools. (Section 613(e)(1)(B))

- Providing direct services to disabled children in charter schools is among the authorized activities for the newly created special subgrants to LEAs under the grants to states program. The 1997 Amendments require a SEA to make

---

[27] The Senate and House committee reports accompanying P.L. 105-17 state that charter schools are expected to be in full compliance with Part B of IDEA.

special IDEA sub-grants to LEAs when its allotment under the grants to states program increases by a certain amount. LEAs are required to use these special sub-grants for capacity building to improve outcomes for children with disabilities. Among the enumerated uses of these sub-grants is providing services for children in charter schools. This provision is intended to ensure disabled students in charter schools have access to IDEA resources. (Section 611(f)(A)(i))

- SEAs must include representatives of charter schools on their IDEA advisory panels. This provision is intended to give charter schools a voice in the review and development of state policy on special education. (Section 612(a)(21)(B)(viii))

A revision in P.L. 105-17 that was not directly aimed at charter schools but potentially will have a significant effect on them is a change in the substate formula under the grants to states program. Assistance is distributed according to formula among and within states. Under prior law, SEAs were prevented from making IDEA awards to LEAs if the grant would otherwise be less than $7,500. This provision effectively cut off many LEA charter schools from IDEA aid. Under the 1997 IDEA Amendments, this provision is dropped. Thus, LEA charter schools no longer need to reach a certain threshold before receiving an IDEA grant.

ED's final regulations for the IDEA, as amended by P.L. 105-17, were released on March 12, 1999.[28] The final regulations clarified and elaborated on the following with respect to charter schools:

- The definition of an LEA includes "a public charter school that is established as an LEA under State law."[29]
- Children with disabilities attending charter schools that are **schools of an LEA** must be served in the same manner as children with disabilities in other schools in the LEA and that funds under Part B of IDEA provided to those charter schools must be provided in the same manner as Part B funds are provided in other schools in the LEA.[30]

---

[28] 64 F.R. 12405 (March 12, 1999).
[29] 34 C.F.R. §300.18.
[30] 34 C.F.R. §300.241.

- Children with disabilities attending public charter schools and their parents retain all rights provided under IDEA;[31]
- If the charter school **is an LEA** receiving IDEA funds, the charter school is responsible for ensuring that IDEA requirements are fulfilled, unless state law assigns these responsibilities to another entity.[32]
- If the charter school **is a school in an LEA**, the LEA is responsible for ensuring that IDEA requirements are fulfilled, unless state law assigns these responsibilities to anther entity.[33]
- If the charter school is **neither an LEA nor a school within an LEA**, the SEA has the ultimate responsibility for ensuring that IDEA requirements are fulfilled.[34]

Issues Specific to ESEA Title I, Education for the Disadvantaged

In order to be eligible to receive grants under ESEA Title I, Part A, a LEA or school must have minimum threshold numbers or percentages of children from low-income families. These thresholds differ for LEAs and schools. The minimum for a LEA is at least 10 children from low-income families and these children must constitute at least 2% of the LEA's total school-age population. If a LEA receives a Title I grant, individual schools are generally eligible to receive a share of those funds only if their number or percentage of pupils from low-income families is among the highest in the LEA, or if the percentage is at least above 35%.[35] Thus, the school eligibility threshold varies widely in different LEAs. In many relatively high poverty LEAs, only schools with 50%, 60%, or even higher percentages of their pupils from low-income families are eligible for Title I grants.

When charter schools are treated as separate LEAs, it may be easier for them to qualify for ESEA Title I, Part A, basic grants, the formula under

---

[31] 34 C.F.R. §300.321(a).
[32] 34 C.F.R. §300.321(b).
[33] 34 C.F.R. §300.321(c).
[34] 34 C.F.R. §300.321(d).
[35] The specific statutory and regulatory provisions for school eligibility to participate in Title I are relatively
extensive and detailed. For a discussion of these provisions, see CRS Report 94-968, Education for the Disadvantage: Analysis of 1994 ESEA Title I Amendments Under P.L. 103-382, by Wayne Riddle. p. 29-30.

which the majority of Title I funds are allocated.[36] When treated as separate LEAs, the relatively low LEA eligibility thresholds described above apply to individual charter schools. Thus, such charter schools may qualify for basic grants even if their number and percentage of pupils from low-income families are quite low.

In contrast, depending on the distribution of pupil poverty rates and numbers among the schools of different LEAs, other public schools (including charter schools that are *not* treated as separate LEAs) generally must meet much higher thresholds in order to qualify for Title I basic grants. Thus, it is likely to be much easier for a charter school to qualify for a Title I basic grant if treated as a separate LEA than as a school in a "regular" LEA.

In contrast, it may be more difficult for charter schools treated as separate LEAs to qualify for grants under the second currently-funded ESEA Title I, Part A formula – concentration grants. In general, a LEA may receive concentration grants only if it is in a county meeting either of the thresholds of 6,500 children from low-income families or a low-income child percentage of 15%, *and* if the LEA itself also meets one of these thresholds. If a LEA receives concentration grant funds, then these funds are combined with the LEA's basic grants, and distributed jointly to schools meeting the same eligibility criteria as for basic grants (described above).

A charter school treated as a separate LEA may be eligible for a concentration grant if it meets the 6,500/15% eligibility criteria, and is in a county meeting one of these criteria. The 15% criterion may not be especially difficult for charter schools to meet, and may be substantially below the eligibility standard for basic grants in many high-poverty urban or rural LEAs. However, no charter school is likely to meet the 6,500 child criterion. There may be cases of charter schools meeting neither the 6,500 nor the 15% threshold, and therefore not eligible to receive concentration grant funds, but they would be eligible if considered to be part of the "regular" LEA in which they are located.

Charter schools have no geographic service boundaries; however, all Title I allocation formulas, especially concentration grants, are geographically based – grants are determined by the number of children in low-income families *and* the percentage these children represent of the total school-age population in the LEA where they reside. Beginning with the 1999-2000 school year (FY1999), Title I, Part A grants are calculated

---

[36] In FY1999, approximately 85% of ESEA Title, Part A funds were allocated as basic grants, the remainder as concentration grants (which are discussed further below).

nationwide by ED on the basis of LEAs; rather than the previous procedure under which ED calculated grants by county, then SEAs determined sub-county allocations to LEAs. Charter schools, whether or not they are treated as separate LEAs under state law, are *not* treated as LEAs by ED in this process, because there are no direct means by which ED can determine the number of "census poverty" children attending charter schools, which "regular" LEAs they came from (where population counts must be reduced), or the total school-age population with which they should be compared to determine the low-income child rate. Thus, ED's Title I grant calculations for 1999-2000 included only traditional, geographically-based LEAs, leaving to SEAs to sort out what funds should be shifted to charter school LEAs.

Additional Issues Involving Multiple Federal Programs

Additional problems or issues that have arisen with respect to federal aid programs and charter schools are discussed below. These issues affect charter school participation in multiple federal programs, including but not limited to the IDEA and/or ESEA Title I.

Data Requirements for Making Grants under Title I, IDEA, and other Federal Programs, Especially for the First Year of School Operations

Many new charter schools are being initiated each year. Without prior year enrollment data, it is very difficult to determine the amount of the grant, if any, for which they would be eligible under ESEA Title, the IDEA, and other federal programs. Thus, states may be forced to use indirect methods to estimate grants, or in some cases may have prohibited schools from receiving funds under these programs in their initial year of operation. For example, Arizona used projected enrollment data to provide ESEA Title grants to 10 new charter schools in 1995-1996, but found that ultimate, actual enrollments were significantly different from the projections. The state later discontinued this practice, requiring schools to have had previous year enrollments in order to receive Title I grants.

In recent years, Minnesota has provided some Title I "reallocation" funds to eligible charters in their first year of operation. These "reallocation" funds are amounts returned from previous year grants because they exceeded the maximum 15% share of Title I funds that a LEA may carry over from one year to the next. These funds previously were simply reallocated to other eligible LEAs statewide. However, this is unlikely to be a satisfactory long-term solution to the first year grant problem for charter schools, in part because LEAs are more frequently meeting the 15% carryover limit, and in part because of the growth in the number of new charter schools each year. Further, this partial and temporary solution has been available only for Title I grants; no IDEA funds have been provided to Minnesota charters in their first year of operation.

Recently published ED "non-regulatory" guidance provides additional examples of ways in which SEAs and LEAs may attempt to provide ESEA Title I grants to charter schools in their initial year of operation. However, this guidance does not require that such first-year grants be provided to charter schools, or any other type of public school, under ESEA Title I or other ED programs. The "first-year grant problem" has long existed with respect to receipt of federal education aid for schools of all types. It was rarely a focus of attention in the past, since the number of newly established public schools each year was relatively small. The existence and rapid growth of charter schools has caused this problem to be considered to be more urgent to many to many simply because of the relatively large number of new charter schools established during each of the last few years. This is an issue that the Congress may wish to consider at greater length in the future with respect to all public schools, not just charter schools.

As was noted earlier, the 1998 amendments to the PCS legislation require ED and SEAs, at least in states receiving PCS grants, to assure that charter schools receive federal aid for which they are eligible, beginning in their first year of operations. These new requirements are to be met within 6 months of the enactment of P.L. 105-278 (which occurred on October 22, 1998).

Administrative Burdens

Each of the state-administered federal education programs has a number of reporting, accountability, and other administrative requirements that must be met by LEAs participating in the program.[37] These requirements were generally devised under an implicit assumption that they would generally be applied to multiple-school LEAs with a central administrative staff (although

---

[37] Occasionally, current law reduces or eliminates these requirements for certain LEAs, especially LEAs of small enrollment size. For example, the ESEA Title I requirements regarding selection of participating schools (ESEA Section 1113(a)) are waived for LEAs with fewer than 1,000 enrolled pupils.

even many conventional LEAs are quite small[38] and may have few schools and limited administrative staff). Charter schools that are treated as separate LEAs are likely to have fewer administrative staff than all but the smallest of "regular" LEAs. In fact, some small charter schools have virtually no full-time administrative staff.

There may be a range of alternative ways to relieve charter schools of some of these administrative responsibilities or to help them meet the requirements. These may include the following:

- Charter schools might be explicitly authorized, and encouraged to contract for administrative services by the "regular" LEA serving the area in which the charter school is located, or by the SEA, other state entity, an intermediate educational agency (where these exist), or non-government consultants.[39]

- SEAs or "regular" LEAs might be required (as a condition of their receipt of federal funds) to provide technical assistance and/or administrative services to charter schools. The Comprehensive ESEA Technical Assistance Centers might also be required to pay particular attention to the needs of charter schools for such assistance.

- The current waiver authority in the Public Charter Schools program statute (ESEA, Title X, Part C, Section 10304(e)) might be more widely used, or at least information on possibilities for waiving federal regulations for charter schools under the current authority might be more broadly disseminated.

- A variety of federal program requirements might be waived for all LEAs with low enrollment, whether they are charter schools or conventional LEAs.

- Charter schools might be explicitly authorized to use a share of the funds they receive under federal programs to meet administrative requirements as well as to serve pupils. Actually, the share of federal program funds that can be used for LEA-level administration is not limited under many

---

[38] In 1994-1995, 21.5% of all LEAs in the Nation had total enrollments of fewer than 300 pupils; however, these LEAs enrolled only 1.0% of all pupils. Similarly, 26.3% of all LEAs, enrolling 5.3% of all pupils, had enrollment of 300-999 pupils.

[39] Several charter schools contract with consultants for the performance of some administrative tasks associated with participation in federal or state aid programs.

programs currently. However, an emphasis on this approach would have the disadvantage of reducing the level of funds available for pupil services.

• All requirements for relevant federal aid programs might be reviewed, and those that are deemed to be least appropriate to apply to charter schools might be waived for such schools.[40]

As was noted above, the 1998 amendments to the PCS statute contain new provisions that charter school administrators and teachers are to be consulted by ED when the Department develops regulations affecting the PCS program or charter school participation in other federal education programs; and requiring ED and SEAs to attempt to minimize the paperwork burdens for charter schools of participation in federal education aid programs. It remains to be seen how, and with what effect, these new provisions will be implemented.

Unwillingness to Participate

Because of difficulties such as those described above, charter schools in states where they are treated as separate LEAs may choose not to participate in federal assistance programs for which they would be eligible. For example, SEA staff in Minnesota stated that some charter schools eligible for ESEA Title I grants do not apply for them, in part to avid the accompanying administrative responsibilities.

Ignorance of Program Provisions or Requirements on the Part of Charter School Staff

Primarily with respect to the IDEA, there is concern that charter school operators are frequently unaware of the requirements of federal law, and may be unwittingly in violation of IDEA requirements. To address this potential problem, SEAs in Arizona and Minnesota, for example, have conducted seminars for charter school administrators to educate them on their responsibilities under the IDEA. Some schools in these and other states have also contracted with consultants who specialize in such areas of IDEA compliance.

---

[40] The ESEA Title I requirement exemptions in the District of Columbia charter school legislation (P.L. 104-134) are an example of this approach.

In many cases, charter schools may be effectively ignorant of grant possibilities not because of lack of information but rather by the opposite problems – an overwhelming amount of information and insufficient staff to sift through it. Charter schools treated as LEAs may receive so many notices of grants and other funding opportunities that they are unable to which of them are worth pursuing.

GENERAL ISSUES REGARDING CHARTER SCHOOLS

This section provides brief analysis of several key issues that have arisen regarding charter schools.

Role of Charter Schools in School Reform Efforts

Charter schools are presently attracting substantial attention because they combine at least four elements that are common to several school reform efforts and strategies that are currently being debated in many states and localities. They are schools of choice, open to enrollment by pupils of the relevant grade level and interests throughout the LEA, or in many cases that state, in which they are located. Another common theme of many current school reform proposals is regulatory flexibility. Charter schools are released from a (varying) range of state and local regulations, and are therefore primary examples of regulatory flexibility in practice. A related theme of several contemporary school reform strategies is outcome accountability. This is also a component of the charter school concept, although (as is discussed below) it is perhaps the least developed one thus far. A final common element to many current education reform proposals is entrepreneurial innovation by teachers and other school staff. This is also quite consistent with the charter school concept, with its emphasis on initiative taken by school founders and staff.

While charter schools are consistent with several elements of numerous current school reform efforts, their limitations should be kept in mind as well. As noted earlier, charter schools are a fast-growing but relatively recent phenomenon. A majority of the schools in operation are in a small number of states, and most of the schools have been open for a relatively short period of time. It is currently unclear how widely charter schools will spread, or how effective they will be in improving pupil outcomes. Further, a few of the charter schools that have been established have experienced financial or governance difficulties that have resulted in closure of the schools relatively soon after they began operations.[41] Some have also raised questions regarding the qualifications of some successful charter school applicants or the adequacy of state and local oversight of charter schools.[42]

Start-Up Problems

The literature on charter school implementation identifies a number of factors that appear to affect the successful initial implementation of charter schools. A survey of charter school developers regarding barriers to developing and implementing charter schools, conducted as part of ED's *A National Study of Charter Schools: Third Year Report*, found the following problems to be cited most frequently: lack of start-up funds (cited by 55% of developers), inadequate operating funds (41%), lack of planning time (37%), inadequate facilities (36%), and state or local board opposition (21%). In contrast, federal regulations were cited as a barrier by only 61% of charter school developers.

Many charter schools appear to be operating at a lower expenditure per pupil rate than other local public schools. Although charter schools in some states are entitled to all or nearly all of the operating revenue they would have received or benefited from as regular schools within a public school district (e.g., the charter schools sponsored by local school districts in Arizona receive funds equal at least to the per pupil expenditures of the sponsoring school district), in others, charter schools receive only a portion of those funds (e.g., in Colorado, charter schools receive at least 80% of the state and local per pupil operating revenue of their local school districts, subject to negotiation of a higher percentage in individual charters; also, SEA staff in Minnesota estimate that charters receive an average of approximately 80% as much in operating funds as other public schools in the state). Issues involving the flow of federal funds to charter schools are considered separately above.

Although some charter schools have access to low-cost use of public school or other public buildings (e.g., recreation centers), or former private school buildings, that would otherwise be unused, charter schools generally

---

[41] According to *A National Study of Charter Schools: Third Year Report*, 32 charter schools closed between 1991-1992 and 1997-1998, representing approximately 3% of all charter schools operating during this period.

[42] See, for example, Off to Market. *Education Week*, April 19, 1997. p. 34-39.

have substantial difficulty in obtaining and paying for appropriate facilities. Few states provide funds for capital expenses (i.e., rent or purchase of facilities and equipment), although some states (e.g., Minnesota) are now providing lease grants to charter schools. Under 1998 amendments to California's charter school law, LEAs are to provide unused school buildings to charter schools at no cost. However, there may be few appropriate facilities immediately available in a locality at any cost. State loan guarantees that are frequently provided to regular LEAs are rarely made available to charter schools, limiting their access to private loan markets to finance the acquisition or renovation of facilities. Frequently, whatever facilities are obtained require substantial renovations, and owners may be loath to invest in these when the short terms of charters (3-5 years in most cases) provide no guarantee of long-term returns on their investment. Arizona has addressed this issue by authorizing 15-year charter terms, although this raises concerns about accountability.

Also, with the exception of such states as Arizona and Minnesota, charter schools typically receive no start-up funding for current operations, which may be important to meet expenses that are incurred before regular operating funds begin to flow. Federal funds, such as those from the federal Public Charter School program (described above) are being used to help pay start-up costs as well.

Few states fund technical assistance for charter schools to help their staff and administrators address the wide range of educational as well as administrative duties and responsibilities that often are not typical for an individual public school. These range from designing a curriculum to administering a budget. Consultants are often available to perform some of these technical functions, albeit at a cost. In Minnesota, the SEA has recently made a grant to the state charter school association, a non-governmental group, to provide certain forms of technical assistance to charter schools, especially (but not only) with respect to IDEA compliance.

Accountability and Outcomes

A key aspect of the charter school concept is that these schools will be held accountable for academic results.[43] From a policy perspective, this

---

[43] Charter schools are also held accountable for proper management and use of public funds. To date, a few charter schools have lost their charters at least in part as a result of financial improprieties. (See: Stecklow, Steve. Arizona Takes the Lead in Charter Schools – For

should involve identification in each school's charter of the academic outcomes that should be attained, determination of how those outcomes will be measured and reported, and delineation of the process through which a charter school will be rewarded for attaining its objectives (i.e., through extension of the charter) or penalized for failing to do so (i.e., termination of the charter).

Several factors appear to complicate the process of holding charter schools accountable for academic results. Although state laws provide for this accountability, Finn, *et al.* in *Charter Schools in Action* report that "most states are still in the developmental state [regarding evaluation of charter schools] and some have still not developed solid accountability and evaluation plans." Some researchers suggest that traditional standardized assessments in use in many states may be inappropriate for gauging the academic progress of students in charter schools that are using non-traditional organization, curricula, and instructional practices.[44] These standardized assessments may be particularly problematic for charters using other kinds of assessments internally to measure student progress, such as performance assessments or portfolios of student work. Another issue is that, reportedly, some school charters contain relatively limited academic objectives and little specification of how progress toward those objectives is to be measured.

Similarly, although one of the primary objectives for the charter school movement is to improve the educational performance of students in these schools, it is still too early to reach any conclusions about the impact charter schools will have on academic achievement. As observed by Finn, *et al.* in *Charter Schools in Action*:

> There is – let us say it plainly and early – one big gap in our (and everyone else's) information base: we do not yet know how much and how well the students in charter schools are learning, or whether their academic achievement will surpass that of similar youngsters enrolled in more conventional schools.

Better or Worse. *Wall Street Journal*. December 24, 1996; and Schmidt, Peter. Citing Debts, L.A. Board Revokes School's Charter. *Education Week*. December 14, 1994.)
[44] Buechler, Charter Schools, p. 35-36.

Political Support for Charter Schools

The charter school concept has attracted support from a wide range of individuals and groups who frequently do not agree on education policy issues or strategies. Several advocates of public schools support charter schools as a preferable alternative to proposals for increased public support of private schools, through vouchers or other mechanisms. Some teachers see charter schools as a means through which they might have increased freedom to use the instructional techniques and materials they consider to be most effective, and to have greater autonomy with respect to a wide range of school policies. Some analysts who emphasize varying pupil needs or parental preferences support the growth of charter schools as a means toward increasing the range of available educational options.

At the same time, some advocates of a maximum degree of school choice, including increased public funding of private schools were feasible, support charter schools as an improvement in this respect over traditional public schools, or as the maximum degree of public support of school choice that is politically feasible, or perhaps as a partial movement toward eventual adoption of public-private school vouchers. Further, some advocates of home schooling support charters as a means whereby public funds may be used to support computer networks or other resources for use in home schools or other independent study programs (as has occurred in California and Michigan).

Nevertheless, others remain opposed to charter schools, at least in their "more" autonomous versions. Teacher organizations sometimes oppose charter school laws that release such schools from general requirements to engage in collective bargaining, or that allow non-certified teachers to work in charter schools. Some individuals fear that widespread establishment of charter schools might lead to increased segregation of pupils by race, economic class, or academic achievement level. In particular, some have been concerned that charter schools will attract primarily relatively advantaged pupils, leaving a disproportionate number of disadvantaged pupils in traditional public schools. However, there is no significant evidence that this is yet occurring in the aggregate.[45]

---

[45] For example, ED's *A National Study of Charter Schools: Third Year Report*, found that overall, pupils enrolled in charter schools have demographic characteristics, including the proportion of economically disadvantaged and limited English proficient pupils, similar to those of the general public school population in the states in which the charter schools are located. Further, the study found that charter schools enroll a disproportionately large number of racial minority pupils in several states (Connecticut, Massachusetts, Michigan, Minnesota, North Carolina, and Texas). However, it was also reported that the proportion

Some public school advocates oppose state laws that allow formerly private schools to be converted into public charter schools, or fear that charter schools are a way station leading to ultimate widespread adoption of public-private school voucher programs. Finally, some are simply concerned about the rapid growth of charter schools in some states (such as Arizona), and/or about the weakness and ambiguity of the accountability provisions of many charter school laws, and fear the unintended consequences of this growth, such as the instability that has resulted from some charter schools closing soon after they began operations.

Effects of Charter Schools on the Conventional Public Schools and LEAs "Left Behind"

Finally, some observers are concerned about the potential impact of charter schools on the conventional public schools and LEAs which charter school pupils leave behind. In many cases, these effects are marginal, as only a very small percentage of pupils leave such conventional public schools to enroll in charter schools. However, in a few localities currently, and potentially many more localities in the future, the effects might be much more substantial. Charter school advocates often argue that the competition provided by charter schools will force public schools to improve their services. However, others are concerned that the loss of pupils and funds may have a less constructive impact on conventional public schools and LEAs, seriously weakening the system for pupils left behind.

It is too soon yet to predict which of these hypotheses is more likely to prove correct. Only one study has thus far been published which focuses specifically on the effects of charter on conventional public school systems.[46] This report is based on case studies in 25 LEAs scattered throughout the Nation. The author concludes, "Typically, school districts had not responded with swift, dramatic improvements at the time of this study. The majority of districts had gone about business-as-usual and responded to charters slowly and in small ways...Certain innovations...had rarely occurred: few superintendents, principals, and teachers in district schools were thinking of charter schools as educational laboratories or were attempting to transfer pedagogical innovations from charters to the district schools, districts were

---

of charter school pupils nationwide with disabilities (8%) was lower than for public school pupils in general (11%).

[46] Rofes, Eric. *How are school districts responding to charter laws and charter schools?* Policy Analysis for California Education. April 1998. 23 p.

still building large school facilities and were rarely creating smaller schools; the large urban districts studied rarely had responded in meaningful ways to charter laws and charter schools."[47] Specific impacts on conventional public schools and LEAs generally included a loss of funds, loss of specific types of students to "niche-focused" charter schools, and increased difficulties in predicting future student enrollment and planning for educational services.

Nevertheless, a minority of about one-quarter of the surveyed LEAs "had responded energetically to the advent of charters and significantly altered their educational programs."[48] "These changes included opening schools organized around a specific philosophy or theme, creating 'add-on' programs such as an after-school program or all-day kindergarten, and offering more diverse activities or curricular resources," as well as efforts to "improve public relations and...to aggressively market their schools to the public."[49]

POLICY OPTIONS FOR THE PUBLIC CHARTER SCHOOLS PROGRAM

Some of the current PCS statutory provisions may be more consistent with the initial, very small, demonstration grant program than with a larger program funded at over $100 million per year. Other issues have arisen during the period since the adoption of this legislation in 1994 that it might not be worthwhile to take into consideration. A selection of possible revisions to the Public Charter Schools legislation are discussed below.

Replace the Current Discretionary Grantmaking Process with an Allocation Formula

Currently, Public Charter School program funds are allocated among states (or schools that apply directly in non-participating states) with acceptable application at the discretion of the Secretary of ED. As was discussed earlier in this report, in determining grant amounts for each participating state (or LEA), the Secretary is to consider both the *selection criteria* that apply to all grants, and the new (in 1998) *priority criteria* that

---

[47] Ibid., p. 2.
[48] Ibid.
[49] ibid., p. 12.

apply to some funds in FY1999-FY2001, and all funds beginning in FY2002. While increasingly complicated, this remains a discretionary/ competitive grant-making process.

Typically, funds are allocated at the Secretary's discretion under ED programs with funding levels below approximately $50-100 million, and are distributed under an allocation formula when programs are funded above this level.[50] Some programs explicitly provide for discretionary awarding of grants at certain appropriation levels, and allocation by formula above this appropriation level.[51] If appropriations continue to increase for the PCS program, the Congress might want to consider amending the statute to provide for an allocation formula. A formula approach has the advantage of further clarifying congressional intent as tot the purpose of the PCS program, as reflected in the fund distribution process. Especially in the case of relatively large programs, the Congress has traditionally chosen to limit administrative discretion, assuming that funds could be most equitably distributed according to an objective formula specified in legislation. In contrast, the primary argument in favor of continuing to provide discretion to ED is that the Secretary could taken into consideration the current statutory *selection and priority criteria*, while maintaining administrative flexibility and perhaps minimizing disruption of current allocation patterns, which have been based on a discretionary process.

If adopted, an allocation formula would presumably be limited to states that have adopted charter school laws, although there are many alternative provisions that might be considered in determining how to allocate funds among these states – e.g., in proportion to total school-age populations (to reflect possible demand for charter schools), in proportion to the number of school-age children in poor families (to reflect both demand for charter schools and ability to pay for them with state and local funds), in proportion to the number of charter schools in operation and the enrollment in them (to reflect immediate need and provide in incentive to establish more schools), etc. Some have suggested that the allocation of federal charter school funds among and within states in proportion to enrollment of high need (disadvantaged, disabled, or limited-English proficient) pupils, or to provide

---

[50] One exception to this pattern is the Bilingual Education program (ESEA Title VII, Part A), which is funded at $160 million for FY1998 for instructional services (Title VII, Part A, Subpart 1), and under which grants are made at the discretion of the Secretary.

[51] For example, the Even Start program (ESEA Title I, Part B) provides for discretionary allocation of appropriations below $50 million, and formula allocation when appropriations are $50 million or above.

special incentives for charter schools that enroll pupils from diverse backgrounds, would be most consistent with the traditional federal role of attempting to provide more equitable educational opportunities for such pupils.[52]

Modify the Regulatory Waiver Authority for Aided Charter Schools

As was noted above, the current charter school waiver authority is potentially broad, but is little used. At the same time, a number of concerns have arisen with respect to participation by charter schools in major federal education assistance programs. It might be worthwhile to consider modifying the waiver authority to require broader dissemination of information about it to states and charter schools, and to more explicitly state that the authority could and should be used to resolve problems or remove barriers that have arisen with respect to participation in the IDEA, ESEA Title I, and other ED programs.

A contrasting potential concern arises from the fact that unlike other regulatory waiver authorities affecting ED programs, there are extremely few limits on the kinds of requirements that may be waived under the Public Charter Schools authority. This authority applies to "any statutory or regulatory requirement over which the Secretary exercises administrative authority except any requirement relating to the elements of a charter school." Based on this language alone, the waiver authority might include several types of requirements that cannot be waived under any other waiver authority affecting ED programs – examples include requirements involving fiscal accountability, parental involvement, civil rights, or IDEA requirements for pupils with disabilities. While it may be unlikely that the current Public Charter Schools waiver authority would be used to waive these types of regulations, such use of the authority is not explicitly prohibited, and some might consider it desirable to add such limitations explicitly, while others might prefer to leave in place the potential authority for waiving these types of requirements.[53]

---

[52] See the testimony of Amy Stuart Wells, professor at the University of California at Los Angeles, before the House Committee on Education and the Workforce, April 9, 1997.

[53] For a more detailed discussion of special waiver and flexibility provisions affecting federal elementary and secondary education programs, see CRS Report 98-676, *Federal Elementary and Secondary Education Programs: Ed-Flex and Other Forms of Flexibility*, by Wayne Riddle.

Clarifying the Intent of the Legislation Regarding Eligibility for Aid of Charter Schools That Were Formerly Private Schools

As noted earlier, charter schools eligible for aid under this program must be "created by a developer as a public school, or...adapted by a developer from an existing public school" (Section 10306(1)(B)). According to ED's "non-regulatory guidance" for the PCS program, "There is no provision nor mechanism in the law for converting private schools into public charter schools" [which would be eligible for aid under this program]. However, the guidance also states that "The ESEA does not foreclose a newly-created public school from using resources previously used by a closed private school or from involving the parents and teachers who may have been involved in the closed private school."[54] In practice, there have apparently been instances where a pre-existing private school has closed, and a newly-created public charter school, which has received assistance under the PCS program, has been established shortly thereafter in the same facility and with many of the same staff and pupils.

Some have expressed concern about assisting formerly private schools converted to public charter schools under this program. Committee and conference reports on the Improving American's Schools Act are not particularly helpful in clarifying the intent of the authors of the legislation on this point. Given the potential for confusion, a clarification of legislative intent might be useful.

If the statute were to be clarified to eliminate schools with any substantial connection to pre-existing private schools from eligibility, some might find such a prohibition to be unnecessary and/or undesirably limiting to states in establishing their charter school programs. While as many as nine states allow the direct conversion of formerly private schools into public charter schools, a restriction against aiding them under this program may be perceived by the affected states and schools as an unwarranted federal intrusion into matters that should be left to state discretion. Another problem, as indicated by ED's guidance cited above, is the practically difficulty of clearly distinguishing between a "direct conversion" of a private school into a pubic charter school versus the creation of a "new" public charter school

---

[54] See *Public Charter Schools Program: Nonregulatory Guidance For-Profit Entities, Private School Conversions, Admissions, and Lotteries.* March 1999. 5 p. Available on the Internet at: [http://www.uscharterschools.org/res_dir/res_primary/fed_gud_pcsp.htm].

which uses the same facility and has many of the same staff and pupils as a pre-existing private school.

Whether or not a school was formerly private, it becomes a public school when it earns charter status. Further, given the lack of a "supplement, not supplant" requirement[55] in the legislation, and the consequent ability of states to transfer funds their own funds among different charter schools, any possible restriction may have little practical effect – federal aid might be allocated to other charter schools in the state, freeing some state funds to be directed to the formerly private schools. Also, there would be an inconsistency between the Public Charter Schools and other ED programs, since the converted schools are eligible for aid under the IDEA, ESEA, etc.

Focus Research on the Development of Accountability Measures for Charter Schools

As was discussed earlier in this report, it seems increasingly clear that accountability provisions are a major point of weakness in the charter school concept and many current school charters. While the mandated evaluation of the Public Charter Schools program is already required to focus on the impact of these schools on pupil achievement, the primary importance of developing and evaluating alternatives for establishing accountability through achievement testing and alternative measures might be emphasized in any future revision of this legislation.[56]

Provide Aid Specifically for Charter School Facilities

As was discussed above, the growth of charter schools in many states has spotlighted problems for many of these schools in obtaining access to appropriate facilities. For a variety of reasons – the relatively short terms of their charters, lack of a designated tax collection base, lack of bonding authority that is typically provided to conventional LEAs, among others – charter schools are generally unable to acquire facilities through purchase or

---

[55] That is, a requirement that federal funds be used only to supplement, and not to supplant (or replace) state and local source funds that would otherwise be available to charter schools.

[56] A study of accountability issues and options for charter schools is currently being undertaken by the Center on Reinventing Public Education, University of Washington, under contract to the U.S. Department of Education. Further information is available on the Internet at: [http://www.uscharterschools.org/tech_assist/ed_initiatives.htm].

construction. Most appear to be leasing space from a variety of public and private sources. In some cases, unused public school or other public buildings, or former private school buildings are made available at rents that vary from virtually no cost to market (i.e., unsubsidized) rental rates. A few states provide grants for leasing of facilities, or make available revolving funds for low-interest loans. Nevertheless, access to adequate facilities at reasonable cost is a substantial and probably increasing problem for charter schools.

While access to facilities is clearly a major problem for charter schools, it may be questioned whether it is appropriate or desirable for the federal government to try to help meet this need. While proposals have been advanced by the Clinton Administration and others for substantial new forms of federal aid for school construction or renovation,[57] such federal aid is currently, and has traditionally been limited to very specific and relatively rare circumstances. In general, limited amounts of funds under some federal education programs may be used for "minor remodeling," but not for more substantial costs of building, renovating, or leasing facilities, or related capital costs.

Nevertheless, if it is deemed appropriate, there are a variety of ways in which the PCS legislation could be modified to provide assistance specifically for acquisition of facilities. The 1998 amendments to the PCS legislation added authority for ED to use a share of the funds reserved for national activities to collect and disseminate "information regarding the financial resources available to charter schools, including access to private capital" (Section 10305(a)(5)). Beyond this relatively limited authority, individual charter schools might be authorized to use any, or some limited portion, of PCS grants to acquire or renovate facilities. Alternately, renewed emphasis might be placed on the current authority for states to establish revolving funds with up to 10% of their PCS grants, and use of those funds to provide low-interest loans to charter schools for acquisition or renovation of facilities might be specifically authorized, in addition, technical assistance, whether offered at the national or state level, might be focused on ways in which charter schools might obtain access to appropriate facilities, including help in obtaining access to private capital markets.

---

[57] See CRS Report 95-1090, *School Facilities Infrastructure: Background and Funding in the 105th Congress*, by Susan Boren.

FUNDING FOR PUBLIC CHARTER SCHOOL FACILITIES: CURRENT FEDERAL POLICY AND H.R. 1

David P. Smole

BACKGROUND

The ability of public charter schools[1] to provide quality educational facilities to their students, teachers, and communities is among the primary factors affecting their success as educational institutions. The quality or adequacy of the facilities that a charter school is able to provide largely depends on available funding that, in turn, is impacted by such factors as characteristics of its state's charter school law, the specific terms of its school charter, state and local economic conditions, and the interaction of these and other factors. The U.S. Department of Education (ED), in *The State of Charter Schools 2000: National Study of Charter Schools – Fourth Year Report*, finds charter school operators reporting that being able to provide adequate facilities ranks high among the challenges they face in implementing their charters and in establishing or continuing their education programs. According to ED's study, three of the top four issues charter school operators cited most often as challenges in implementing their programs involved funding: start-up costs, inadequate operating funds, and

---

[1] For more information on charter schools, see CRS Report 97-519, *Public Charter Schools: State Developments and Federal Policy Options*, by Wayne Riddle and James Stedman.

inadequate facilities.[2] These funding issues often are interrelated in how they apply to facilities, with the adequacy of charter school facilities often dependent upon the availability of funds for start-up costs and the level of funding provided for operating expenses – both of which frequently are used to pay for facilities.

According to ED's The State of Charter Schools 2000, nearly three-quarters of public charter schools begin operations as newly created schools. Operators of these schools must not only implement their new education plans, but also must surmount the obstacle of acquiring adequate facilities in which to house their schools. In addition, many charter schools are designed to be smaller in size than traditional public schools; and oftentimes, charter schools begin operations with only a few of their planned eventual grade levels, intending to add an additional grade level each successive year. These factors often require charter school operators to arrange initially for temporary facilities as they obtain financing for, and acquire, renovate, or build, long-term facilities. Specific difficulties charter school operators face in obtaining adequate facilities include: limited dedicated funds for facilities; lack of available and affordable space; problems in purchasing, leasing, or occupying pre-existing public school facilities; an inability to issue bonds or assume debt; and obtaining adequate facilities financing.

CHARTER SCHOOL FACILITIES IN THE STATES

State Funding

States generally provide charter schools with operational funding on a per-pupil basis – usually a certain percentage of the per-pupil funding provided to other public schools by the state or local school district. A number of states and the federal government also provide some funding for charter school start-up costs. Currently, seven states (Arizona, Colorado, Florida, Massachusetts, Minnesota, Utah, New York) and the District of

---

[2] U.S. Department of Education. Office of Educational Research and Improvement. *The State of Charter Schools 2000: National Study of Charter Schools, Fourth-Year Report*, by Beryl Nelson et al, RPP International, January 2000. pp. 44-45. (Hereafter cited as ED, *The State of Charter Schools 2000*). The report finds that 48.5% of respondents cited start-up costs as a challenge, 37.4% cited inadequate operating funds, 34.5% cited lack of planning time, and 32.0% cited inadequate facilities. In most states, charter school operators must use operating funds to pay for the cost of facilities.

Columbia also provide annual funding for charter school facilities through either per-pupil allocations or through grants.[3] According to ED's *Venturesome Capital: State Charter School Finance Systems*,[4] North Carolina and Rhode Island include capital outlay and/or debt service costs as part of the base operating funding provided to charter schools, while Georgia requires local school districts to share capital funds with charter schools if that is feasible. Charter schools in a few states (Arizona, District of Columbia, and Massachusetts) can use capital funding for operational expenses – a use generally prohibited in the case of conventional public schools. This provides charter schools in these states with greater flexibility in how they manage their cash flow. In contrast, New Jersey prohibits charter schools from using public funds for facilities construction.

When public charter schools were first being considered as alternatives to conventional public schools, in some instances, the rationale for their support was the presumption that charter schools would be able to operate more efficiently and at lower cost than conventional public schools. Occasionally, it also was presumed that some of the financial support for public charter schools might be provided through philanthropy. However, while some schools have been successful in obtaining funding or the use of space from private donors or the business community, many philanthropic organizations have policies prohibiting the use of funds for capital expenses.

Access to Available and Affordable Space

Obtaining access to adequate and affordable space has been a challenge to many public charter schools. As the nation's school age population continues to grow, there continues to be an increasing demand for education facilities. According to the National Center for Education Statistics (NCES), billions of dollars are needed to fund the construction of new schools and large numbers of existing schools are badly in need of repair, with estimated costs for renovation approaching $127 billion.[5] The facility needs of charter

---

[3] Sandham, Jessica L. Some States Help Charter Schools Put a Roof Overhead, *Education Week*, June 20, 2001. p. 23.

[4] U.S. Department of Education. Office of Educational Research and Improvement. *Venturesome Capital: State Charter School Finance Systems*, by F. Howard Nelson, Edward Muir, and Rachel Drown, American Federation of Teachers Educational Foundation. Jessup, MD, December 2000. pp. 128, 165, 172, and 175. (Hereafter cited as ED, *Venturesome Capital*.)

[5] U.S Department of Education. Office of Educational Research and Improvement. National Center for Education Statistics. *Condition of America's Public School Facilities: 1999, Statistical Analysis Report 2000-032*. Washington, D.C., June 2000, p. B-29.

schools are not dissimilar to those of conventional public schools, with the level of need often varying according to geopolitical and socioeconomic factors. A majority of charter schools are concentrated in high growth states or in cities with troubled urban school districts. In high growth states, there is an overall shortage of public school facilities. In these locations, both charter schools and conventional public schools are struggling to obtain new or expanded facilities. Often conventional school districts welcome the arrival of charter schools because they relieve some of the pressure for building new facilities. In urban school districts, it is more likely that existing educational facilities are underutilized; however, often they also are in need of repair or renovation. While charter school operators can sometimes acquire excess facilities in which top operate a charter school, often they must bear the cost of renovation.

In general, the limited amount of funds allocated specifically for facilities and capital expenses has resulted in some charter school operators experiencing difficulty in obtaining adequate school space in which to educate their students, resulting, at least initially, in charter schools being housed in non-conventional or less than desirable facilities.[6] Examples of non-conventional charter school facilities include churches, museums, movie theaters, bowling alleys, farmers' markets, and former commercial or industrial buildings – places where charter school operators have been able to obtain space at affordable rates while they work to secure more adequate facilities. Other charter school facilities include space formerly used by private schools or organizations such as YMCAs and recreation centers.

Pre-Existing Public School Facilities

Depending on characteristics of a state's charter school law and the size of the local school age population, some charter schools are able to obtain facilities from local school districts. Options include converting a pre-existing school to a charter school and retaining use of the building or occupying excess facilities made available by a local school district. Some state charter laws require local school districts to provide charter schools access to excess facilities, either at no expense or for a nominal fee. Other

---

[6] While charter schools are relieved of many education rules and regulations in exchange for increased accountability, they still are required to adhere to Part B of the Individuals with Disabilities Education Act and "all applicable Federal, State, and local health and safety requirements" (20 U.S.C. 8066(1)(G)&(J)).

state laws require school districts to offer charter schools the right of first refusal when existing public school facilities are sold or allow charter schools to purchase public school facilities at a discount. In many instances, the availability of excess public school facilities is strongly correlated with growth or decline in the local school age population. In high growth areas, few, if any, excess school facilities are available and often public school districts are struggling to provide adequate school facilities for their burgeoning student populations. In areas with declining school age populations, excess school facilities often are available, but may be outmoded or poorly maintained.

According to ED's *Venturesome Capital*, school districts in Colorado must provide charter schools with free access to vacant facilities. In the District of Columbia, charter schools can purchase or lease existing public school facilities at a 15-25% discount. In Georgia, while charter schools are not guaranteed specific funding for facilities, school districts are required to provide some capital funding to charter schools when feasible. As most of Georgia's charter schools use pre-existing school facilities, funding for facilities there has not been a serious issue. In Hawaii, all school facilities, including charter schools, are financed by the legislature. Also, all charter schools in Hawaii have been converted from pre-existing schools. In Louisiana and New Mexico, charter schools can negotiate with the local school board to use pre-existing public school facilities. In Kansas, Massachusetts and Wisconsin, many charter schools are housed in existing public school facilities.[7] In Ohio, school districts now are required to provide charter school operators with the first opportunity to purchase excess school facilities that are being sold. These and other examples clearly indicate the extent to which the conditions upon which a charter school may use pre-existing public school facilities vary according to each state's charter school law.

Facility Financing Options

Whereas conventional public schools generally finance the construction or renovation of facilities through local tax levies or the issuance of municipal bonds, in most cases such options are not available to public charter schools. However, most states with charter school laws do allow public charter schools to assume debt for purposes of financing facilities,

---

[7] ED, *Venturesome Capital*, pp. 111, 121, 128, 131, 138, 142, 146-149, 162, and 182-184.

although the entity ultimately responsible for the debt varies from state to state. In some states, the charter school is fully responsible for the debt, whereas in others, the local school district or the chartering authority would become responsible should the charter school become unable to retire the debt.

Aside from who is responsible for charter school debt, the acquisition of debt depends on a number of factors. Lenders decide whether to provide financing, and if so, set the interest rate at which they provide financing, based on their perception of risk. Financial institutions have tended to regard charters schools as risky ventures because of their novelty and uncertainty about their long-term viability. Charter schools still are a relatively new concept in education and lenders do not have much experience working with them. Also, lenders have been reluctant to issue loans for periods exceeding the length of a school's approved charter.[8] Higher interest rates and shorter payments often combine to limit charter schools' opportunities for financing facilities.

To assist charter schools, Arizona, Colorado, Michigan, North Carolina, and Texas specifically authorize their charter schools to issue tax-exempt securities to finance facilities. The ability to issue tax-exempt securities allows a charter school to obtain financing at a lower rate than would otherwise be available on the open market because purchasers of these securities are exempted from paying state income taxes on the interest they earn, and thus accept a lower rate of return.

Other states, including California, Connecticut, Illinois, and Louisiana, make funds available to public charter schools through revolving loan funds. Revolving loan funds may be established by a public or private entity and provide capital to charter schools, usually at a lower interest rate than otherwise might be available. As the loans are repaid, the capital and interest that flow back into the fund become available to make future loans. Revolving loan funds have been used to finance charter school facilities and cover start-up costs. Still, along with all other types of debt, unless a charter school has access to funds specifically allocated for facilities, it must pay off any debt it incurs with a portion of its revenues – usually its operating funds.

---

[8] Charters in most other states are approved for a period of up to 5 years, however, they may be granted for up to 15 years in Arizona, the District of Columbia, and Florida.

FEDERAL POLICY

Existing Policy

The federal government has established itself as a provider of some financial assistance to public charter schools. In response to concerns about charter school start-up costs and the availability of operating funds, the 103rd Congress authorized the federal Public Charter School (PCS) program in 1994 as Title X, Part C of the Elementary and Secondary Education Act (ESEA). The 105th Congress amended and expanded Title X, Part C under the Charter School Expansion Act of 1998. The PCS program provides funding for the design, implementation, and implementation, and evaluation of public charter schools. Appropriations for the PCS program have grown from $6 million in FY1995 to $190 million in FY2001. IN FY1999, ED awarded more than $41 million in new and $54 million in continuation grants either to state educational agencies (SEAs) or directly to charter school in 32 states, the District of Columbia, and Puerto Rico. In FY2000, ED awarded $16.5 million in new and $110 million in continuation grants to benefit charter schools in 36 states, the District of Columbia, and Puerto Rico.[9] The President's FY2002 budget includes a request of $200 million for the PCS program. Charter schools also are eligible for all other federal aid programs on the same basis as other public schools.[10]

As part of the FY2001 Omnibus Appropriations Act (P.L. 106-554), the 106th congress amended the PCS program to address charter school facilities needs by creating the Charter School Facilities Financing Demonstration program. This program will provide a minimum of three competitive grants totaling $25 million to entities (public entity, private non-profit entity, or consortium of each) to assist public charter schools in the acquisition, construction, or renovation of facilities by enhancing availability of loans or bond financing.[11] Grantees of this program will deposit funds from their

---

[9] As of September 17, 2001, ED has awarded $30 million to SEAs or charter schools in Arizona, California, Kansas, Missouri, New Mexico, Nevada, Pennsylvania, Rhode Island, and South Carolina during FY2001. Of this, $12 million have been awarded to charter schools in Arizona.

[10] For more information on how related federal programs apply to public charter schools, see CRS Report 97-519, *Public Charter Schools*, by Wayne Riddle. pp. 13-20.

[11] ED has not yet awarded any charter school facilities financing demonstration grants. ED's request for proposals (RFP) is currently being reviewed by OMB. Upon receipt of OMB approval, ED will publish the RFP in the *Federal Register*, after which applicants will have 45-60 days during which to apply for the grants.

grants into a reserve account and use the funds for one or more of the following purposes:

* Guaranteeing, insuring, and reinsuring bonds, notes, and other debt used to finance charter school facilities.
* Guaranteeing and insuring leases of personal and real property.
* Facilitating charter schools' facilities financing by identifying potential lending sources, encouraging private lending, and other similar activities.
* Facilitating the issuance of bonds by charter schools, or by other public entities for the benefit of charter schools, by providing technical, administrative, and other appropriate assistance (including the recruitment of bond counsel, underwriters, and potential investors and the consolidation of multiple charter school projects within a single bond issue).[12]

ED expects to award between three and five one-time grants under the Charter School Facilities Financing Demonstration program.

In addition, charter schools that are classified as separate LEAs can apply for federal funds for school renovations through their state from a related provision in the FY2001 appropriations legislation, the School Renovation, IDEA, and Technology Grants.[13] Finally, a small number of charter schools have been provided with funding for facilities financing through the Department of Agriculture's Rural Housing Service (RHS) and through Qualified Zone Academy Bonds (QZAB).[14]

---

[12] U.S. Department of Education. *Charter School Facilities Financing Demonstration Program Fact Sheet.* Available from [http://www.ed.gov/inits/construction/charter.html], accessed September 13, 2001.

[13] States are expected to award School Renovation, IDEA, and Technology Grants during the spring of 2002. There are $823 million in emergency renovation funds available to states out of $1.1 billion being distributed through the grants. See also CRS Report RS20171, *School Facilities Infrastructure: Background and Legislative Proposals*, by Susan Boren, for more information.

[14] Government Accounting Office. *Charter Schools: Limited Access to Facility Financing.* Washington, D.C., September 2000. pp. 15-16. See also CRS Report RS20699, *Funding School Renovation: Qualified Zone Academy Bonds vs. Traditional Tax-Exempt Bonds*, by Steven Maguire.

Current Proposals, 107th Congress: H.R. 1

The Senate version of H.R. 1, the Better Education for Students and Teachers Act, contains an amendment cited as the Charter Schools Equity Act (§5168), the purposes of which are:

[A] to help eliminate the barriers that prevent charter school developers from accessing the credit markets, by encouraging lending institutions to lend funds to charter schools on terms more similar to the terms typically extended to traditional public schools; and

[B] to encourage the States to provide support to charter schools for facilities financing in an amount more nearly commensurate to the amount the States have typically provided for traditional public schools.

The Senate version of H.R. 1 authorizes "Per-Pupil Facilities Aid Programs" (§51151(b)) which would make funds available for grants to States to "establish or enhance, and administer, a per-pupil facilities aid program for charter schools in the State." These programs would be authorized at $200 million for FY2002 and for such sums as may be necessary in subsequent years.

The Per-Pupil Facilities Aid programs would provide funding on a competitive basis to states whose laws provide for the annual financing of charter school facilities on a per-pupil basis and require that such financing also must be dedicated solely for facilities. Funds would be provided on a sliding scale over time, with states receiving no more than 90% of the cost of the program in the first year of the program, declining to no more than 20% of the cost of the program in the fifth year.

This amendment would provide those states whose charter school laws complied with the requirements of the act with access to supplemental per-pupil funding for facilities. While this report does not identify which states currently would qualify for grants under the Per-Pupil Facilities Aid program, it appears, based on descriptions found in ED's report,[15] that relatively few current charter school states would be eligible. As noted earlier in this report, only a small number of states provide annual charter school facilities funding on a per-pupil basis, and among those that do, some

---

[15] ED, *Venturesome Capital.*

allow facilities funding to be used for general operating expenses, which would disqualify them from the program.

The prospect of providing states the opportunity to apply for competitive grants for per-pupil facilities funding might encourage states to modify their state charter school laws so that they would comply with the requirements of the Per-Pupil Facilities Aid programs (i.e., providing per-pupil facilities funding and adding restrictions to charter schools' use of such funds). Consequences of doing so include providing public charter schools with needed facilities funding, but with strings attached – the creation of additional restrictions on the use of such funds.

The Charter Schools Equity Act also contains an amendment called, "Credit Enhancement Initiatives to Promote Charter School Facility Acquisition, Construction, and Renovation" (§§5126-5126J). This amendment closely parallels the Charter School Facilities Financing Demonstration program discussed above, except that it is proposed to be funded annually at $200 million, beginning with FY2002, whereas the demonstration program has a one-time appropriation of $25 million. ED has not yet granted funds under the Charter Schools Facilities Financing Demonstration program, however, so no information presently is available regarding its implementation or effectiveness. Nevertheless, it seems likely that the effects of the current proposal would be, at a minimum, to increase the scale of the demonstration and establish it for a longer time period.

Finally, an amendment to provide authorization for the use of federal matching funds for school construction to assist in the reduction of school size is included under the Innovative Education Program Strategies of Title V of the Senate version of H.R.1 (§§5351-5354).[16] Funds made available under this amendment could be used by any public school, rather than specifically begin targeted to charter schools. However, the funding level per pupil would likely be very small. Further, if adopted, this would be one of many authorized uses of funds under this program. Thus, the impact of this provision on charter schools *per se* might be limited.

---

[16] For further information on school construction issues contained in H.R. 1, see CRS Report RS20171, *School Facilities Infrastructure: Background and Legislative Proposals*, by Susan Boren.

SELECTED BIBLIOGRAPHY

1996-97 report to the House and Senate committees on education: a description of Michigan public school academies (charter schools) / State of Michigan, Department of Education. Published/Created: Lansing, Mich. (P.O. Box 30008, Lansing 48909): The Department, [1999] Related Authors: Michigan. Dept. of Education. Description: 1 v. (various pagings): ill.; 30 cm. Notes: "Received by the Michigan State Board of Education, February 18, 1999." Subjects: Charter schools--Michigan--Directories. Privatization in education--Michigan. Education--Demographic aspects--Michigan. LC Classification: LB2806.36 .A25 1999 Dewey Class No.: 371.01/025/774 21

A national study of charter schools: second-year report / RPP International; Paul Berman ... [et al.]. Published/Created: Washington, DC: Office of Educational Research and Improvement, U.S. Dept. of Education: For sale by the U.S. G.P.O., Supt. of Docs., 1998. Related Authors: Berman, Paul, 1937- United States. Office of Educational Research and Improvement. RPP International. Description: x, 130 p.: ill.; 28 cm. ISBN: 0160497523 Notes: "Funded by the U.S. Department of Education"--T.p. verso. "July 1998"--T.p. verso. "SAI 98-3033"--P. 4 of cover. Additional Form Avail.: Online version available at the Department's home page. Subjects: Charter schools--United States. Charter schools--United States--Statistics. LC Classification: LB2806.36 .N39 1998 Dewey Class No.: 371.01 21

A study of charter school accountability: national charter

school accountability study / Paul
Hill ... [et al.] (Center on
Reinventing Public Education,
Daniel J. Evans School of Public
Affairs, University of
Washington).
Published/Created: [Washington,
D.C.]: Office of Educational
Research and Improvement, U.S.
Dept. of Education; Jessup, MD:
U.S. Dept. of Education, ED Pubs
[distributor, 2001]
Related Authors: Hill, Paul
Thomas, 1943- Daniel J. Evans
School of Public Affairs. Center
on Reinventing Public Education.
Description: x, 87, A-10 p.: ill.;
28 cm.
Notes: "June 2001"--T.p. verso.
"SAI 2001-3000"--P. [4] of cover.
Includes bibliographical
references.
Subjects: Charter schools--United
States--Evaluation. Educational
accountability--United States.
LC Classification: LB2806.36
.S75 2001

A study of charter schools: first-year
report, 1997 / RPP International
and the University of Minnesota.
Published/Created: [Washington,
D.C.]: U.S. Dept. of Education,
Office of Educational Research
and Improvement, [1997]
Related Authors: University of
Minnesota. Center for Applied
Research and Educational
Improvement. RPP International.
United States. Office of
Educational Research and

Improvement.
Description: vi, 74 p.: ill.; 28 cm.
Notes: " A collaborative effort of
... RPP International and CAREI
of the University of Minnesota"--
Pref. "May 1997"--T.p. verso.
Includes bibliographical
references. Additional Form
Avail.: Online version available
at:
http://www.ed.gov/pubs/charter/
Subjects: Charter schools--United
States. Education and state--
United States.
LC Classification: LB2806.36
.S78 1997
Dewey Class No.: 371.01 21

Alberta Education.
Charter school handbook / Alberta
Education.
Published/Created: Edmonton,
Alta.: Alberta Education, [1995]
Description: iii, 34 leaves: ill.; 28
cm. ISBN: 0773217681
Notes: Cover title. "April 1995."
Errata sheet inserted.
Subjects: Charter schools--
Alberta. Educational planning--
Alberta. School management and
organization--Alberta.
LC Classification: LB2806.36
.A53 1995

Barr, Robert D.
How to create alternative, magnet,
and charter schools that work /
Robert D. Barr and William H.
Parrett.
Published/Created: Bloomington,
Ind.: National Educational

Service, 1997.
Related Authors: Parrett, William.
Description: xiv, 231 p.; 23 cm.
ISBN: 1879639483
Notes: Includes bibliographical
references.
Subjects: Alternative schools--
United States. Magnet schools--
United States. Charter schools--
United States.
LC Classification: LC46.4 .B37
1997
Dewey Class No.: 371.04/0973 21

Birkett, Frederick A.
Charter schools: the parent's
complete guide: everything you
need to know to make the right
decision for your child / Frederick
A. Birkett.
Published/Created: Roseville,
Calif.: Prima Pub., c2000.
Description: xvii, 237 p.: ill.; 22
cm. ISBN: 0761525165
Notes: Includes bibliographical
references (p. 225-226) and index.
Subjects: Charter schools--United
States. School choice--United
States.
LC Classification: LB2806.36
.B47 2000
Dewey Class No.: 371.01 21

Blakemore, Catherine.
A public school of your own: your
guide to creating and running a
charter school / Catherine
Blakemore.
Published/Created: Golden, Colo.:
Adams-Pomeroy Press, c1998.
Description: xii, 227 p.; 22 cm.
ISBN: 0966100913

Notes: Includes bibliographical
references (p. 182-188) and index.
Subjects: Charter schools--United
States. School management and
organization--United States.
LC Classification: LB2806.36
.B53 1998
Dewey Class No.: 371.04 21

Bonsteel, Alan, 1951-
A choice for our children: curing
the crisis in America's schools /
Alan Bonsteel and Carlos A.
Bonilla; with an exchange of
views between John E. Coons and
Milton Friedman; and with
contributions by James Horsman
and Stephen D. Sugarman.
Published/Created: San Francisco:
ICS Press, c1997.
Related Authors: Bonilla, Carlos
A.
Description: xv, 256 p.: ill., map;
23 cm. ISBN: 1558154965 (pb)
Notes: Includes bibliographical
references and index.
Subjects: School choice--United
States. School choice--California-
-Case studies. Charter schools--
United States. Charter schools--
California--Case studies.
Educational vouchers--United
States. Educational vouchers--
California--Case studies.
LC Classification: LB1027.9 .B65
1997
Dewey Class No.: 379.1/11/0973
21

Caldwell, Russell B.
Colorado charter schools capital
finance study: challenges and

opportunities for the future /
prepared by Russell B. Caldwell
and Barry Arrington for Colorado
Department of Education.
Published/Created: Denver, CO
(201 E. Colfax Ave., Denver
80203): The Department, 2000.
Related Authors: Arrington,
Barry. Colorado. Dept. of
Education.
Description: 43, 6, 9, 5 p.; 28 cm.
Notes: "January 2000." Cover
title. Additional Form Avail.:
4/4/2000: Also available via
Internet.
Subjects: Charter schools--
Colorado--Finance.
LC Classification: LB2806.36
.C35 2000
Govt. Doc. No.:
ED2.2/C38/2000/2 codocs

Carrasco, Joe.
Public school academies in
Michigan / by Joe Carrasco, Jr.,
Kathryn Summers-Coty.
Published/Created: Lansing,
Mich.: Senate Fiscal Agency,
[2000]
Related Authors: Summers-Coty,
Kathryn. Michigan. Legislature.
Senate. Fiscal Agency.
Description: 16 p.; 28 cm.
Notes: Cover title. "October
2000." "A series of papers
examining critical issues facing
the Michigan Legislature."
Subjects: Charter schools--Law
and legislation--Michigan.
Educational change--Michigan.
Series: Issue papers (Michigan.

Legislature. Senate. Fiscal
Agency)
Variant Series: Issue paper
LC Classification: LB2806.36
.C37 2000
Dewey Class No.: 371.01 21

Challenge and opportunity: the impact
of charter schools on school
districts / RPP International; John
Ericson ... [et al.].
Published/Created: [Washington,
D.C.]: Office of Educational
Research and Improvement, U.S.
Dept. of Education: For sale by
the Supt. of Docs., U.S. G.P.O.,
[2001]
Related Authors: Ericson, John.
RPP International.
Description: vi, 55 p.: ill.; 28 cm.
ISBN: 016050855X
Notes: "June 2001"--T.p. verso.
Includes bibliographical
references (p. 54-55).
Subjects: Charter schools--United
States--Evaluation. School
districts--United States--
Evaluation. Charter schools--
United States--Statistics. School
districts--United States--Statistics.
LC Classification: LB2806.36
.C515 2001
Dewey Class No.: 371.01 21

Charter school progress report: NRS
386.500: educational
performance, fiscal analysis, and
NRS 386.600(1)(a) reports.
Published/Created: [Carson City,
Nev.?: Dept. of Education?, 2001]
Related Authors: Nevada. Dept.

of Education.
Description: 1 v. (various pagings): ill.; 28 cm.
Notes: Cover title. "February 1, 2001."
Subjects: Charter schools--Nevada--Evaluation. Charter schools--Nevada--Statistics.
LC Classification: LB2806.36 .C52 2001
Dewey Class No.: 371.01 21

Charter schools / [edited by] Thomas Murphy.
Published/Created: Huntington, NY: Nova Science Publishers, 2002.
Projected Pub. Date: 0202
Related Authors: Murphy, Thomas (Thomas Zacharaiah)
Description: p. cm. ISBN: 1590331966
Notes: Includes index.
Subjects: Charter schools.
LC Classification: LB2806.36 .C535 2002
Dewey Class No.: 371.01 21

Charter schools information packet: the Colorado Charter Schools Act of 1993.
Published/Created: Denver, Colo.: Colorado Dept. of Education, [1993]
Related Authors: Colorado. Dept. of Education. Colorado. Charter Schools Act.
Description: 44 p.; 28 cm.
Notes: Cover title. "September 1993." Includes text of the Colorado Charter Schools Act, 1993. Includes bibliographical references (p. 41-44).
Subjects: Educational law and legislation--Colorado. Charter schools--Colorado. School management and organization--Parent participation Law and legislation--Colorado. Charter schools--Colorado.
LC Classification: KFC2190.A339 A2 1993
Dewey Class No.: 344.788/071 347.880471 20
Govt. Doc. No.: ED2.2/C38/1993 codocs

Charter schools: a comprehensive overview.
Published/Created: Albany, N.Y.: University of the State of New York, State Education Dept., Office for Planning, Research and Support Services, [1994]
Related Authors: University of the State of New York. Office for Planning, Research, and Support Services.
Description: v, 66 p.; 28 cm.
Notes: "January 1994." Includes bibliographical references (p. 63-66).
Subjects: Charter schools--United States. Charter schools--New York (State) School management and organization--United States. School management and organization--New York (State) School improvement programs--United States. School improvement programs--New York (State)
LC Classification: LB1029.F7 C43 1994

Dewey Class No.: 371/.04/0973 20
Govt. Doc. No.: UNI,617-4,CHASC,94-26218 nydocs

Charter schools: lessons in school reform / edited by Liane Brouillette.
Published/Created: Mahwah, N.J.: L. Erlbaum Associates, 2002.
Projected Pub. Date: 0111
Related Authors: Brouillette, Liane, 1947-
Description: p. cm. ISBN: 0805837248 (cloth: alk. paper)
Notes: Includes bibliographical references and indexes.
Subjects: Charter schools--United States. Educational change--United States.
LC Classification: LB2806.36 .C54 2002
Dewey Class No.: 371.01 21

Charters, vouchers, and public education / Paul E. Peterson and David E. Campbell, editors.
Published/Created: Washington: Brookings Institution Press, c2001.
Projected Pub. Date: 0109
Related Authors: Peterson, Paul E. Campbell, David E., 1971-
Description: p. cm. ISBN: 081577026X (cloth: alk. paper) 0815770278 (pbk.: alk. paper)
Notes: Includes biblographical references and index.
Subjects: Charter schools--United States. Educational vouchers--United States.

LC Classification: LB2806.36 .C55 2001
Dewey Class No.: 371.01 21

Colorado charter school information packet and handbook: the Colorado Charter Schools Act of 1993.
Edition Information: 7th ed.
Published/Created: Denver, Colo.: Colorado Dept. of Education, 1999.
Related Authors: Colorado. Dept. of Education. Colorado. Charter Schools Act.
Description: 1 v. (various pagings): ill.; 28 cm.
Notes: Cover title. "September 1999." Includes text of the Colorado Charter Schools Act. Includes bibliographical references. Additional Form Avail.: 10/28/99: Also available via the Internet.
Subjects: Charter schools--Law and legislation--Colorado. Charter schools--Colorado.
Govt. Doc. No.: ED2.2/C38/1999 codocs

Colorado charter school information packet and handbook: the Colorado Charter Schools Act of 1993.
Edition Information: 5th ed.
Published/Created: Denver, Colo. (201 East Colfax Ave., Denver 80203): Colorado Dept. of Education, [1997]
Related Authors: Colorado. Dept. of Education. Colorado. Charter

Schools Act.
Description: 1 v. (various pagings): ill.; 28 cm.
Notes: Cover title. "September 1997." Includes text of the Colorado Charter Schools Act. Includes bibliographical references.
Subjects: Charter schools--Law and legislation--Colorado. Charter schools--Colorado.
LC Classification: KFC2191.C57 C65 1997
Dewey Class No.: 344.788/071 21
Govt. Doc. No.: ED2.2/C38/1997/2 codocs

Colorado charter school information packet and handbook: the Colorado Charter Schools Act of 1993 / editor, William Windler.
Edition Information: 6th ed.
Published/Created: Denver, Colo. (201 East Colfax Ave., Denver 80203): Colorado Dept. of Education, 1998.
Related Authors: Windler, William. Colorado. Dept. of Education.
Description: 1 v. (various pagings): ill.; 28 cm.
Notes: Cover title.
Subjects: Charter schools--Law and legislation--Colorado. Charter schools--Colorado.
LC Classification: KFC2191.C57 C65 1998
Dewey Class No.: 344.788/071 21
Govt. Doc. No.: ED2.2/C38/1998 codocs

Colorado charter schools evaluation study / prepared by the Clayton Foundation for the Colorado Department of Education.
Published/Created: Denver, Colo.: The Department,
Related Authors: Clayton Foundation for Research. Colorado. Dept. of Education.
Description: v.; 28 cm.
Cancel/Invalid LCCN: 98162687 99205659
Notes: Description based on: 1997; title from cover. Issued by the Clayton Foundation, 1997-1998.
Subjects: Charter schools--Colorado--Evaluation--Periodicals.
LC Classification: LB2806.36 .C653
Connecticut. State Board of Education.
Report on the operation of the charter schools.
Published/Created: [Hartford]: Connecticut State Board of Education, [2000-
Description: v.; 28 cm. Vol. for 1997-98 also contains data for 1998-99 and 1999-2000. 1997-98-
Current Frequency: Annual
Notes: "In accordance with Section 10-66gg of the Connecticut General Statutes ..."--Letter of transmittal. Title from cover.
Subjects: Charter schools--Connecticut--Periodicals. Charter schools--Connecticut--Finance--Periodicals. Educational law and legislation--Connecticut--Periodicals. Parent-teacher

relationships--Connecticut--
Periodicals.
LC Classification: LB2806.36
.C67a

Engel, Michael, 1944-
The struggle for control of public
education: market ideology vs.
democratic values / Michael
Engel.
Published/Created: Philadelphia,
Pa.: Temple University Press,
c2000.
Description: xi, 223 p.; 22 cm.
ISBN: 1566397405 (cloth: alk.
paper) 1566397413 (pbk.: alk.
paper)
Notes: Includes bibliographical
references and index.
Subjects: Public schools--United
States. Politics and education--
United States. Education--
Economic aspects--United States.
School choice--United States.
Charter schools--United States.
LC Classification: LA217.2 .E533
2000
Dewey Class No.: 371.01/0973 21

Felton, Keith Spencer.
Indispensable tools: a principal
builds his high school: dialogues
on charter education with Peter
Thorp / Keith Spencer Felton.
Published/Created: Lanham, MD:
University Press of America,
2001.
Projected Pub. Date: 0105
Related Authors: Thorp, Peter.
Description: p. cm. ISBN:
0761820159 (pbk.: alk. paper)

Notes: Includes index.
Subjects: Thorp, Peter--
Interviews. High school
principals--United States--
Interviews. Charter schools--
United States--Case studies.
LC Classification: LB2831.92
.F45 2001
Dewey Class No.: 373.12/012 21

Finn, Chester E., 1944-
Charter schools in action:
renewing public education /
Chester E. Finn, Bruno V. Manno,
Gregg Vanourek.
Published/Created: Princeton,
N.J.: Princeton University Press,
c2000.
Related Authors: Manno, Bruno
V. Vanourek, Gregg.
Description: x, 290 p.; 25 cm.
ISBN: 0691004803 (cloth: alk.
paper)
Notes: Includes bibliographical
references and index.
Subjects: Charter schools--United
States.
LC Classification: LB2806.36
.F527 2000
Dewey Class No.: 371.01 21

Fiore, Thomas A.
Charter schools and students with
disabilities: review of existing
data, 1998 / Thomas A. Fiore,
Sandra H. Warren, Erin R.
Cashman.
Published/Created: Washington,
DC: Office of Educational
Research and Improvement, U.S.
Dept. of Education, [1999]

Related Authors: Warren, Sandra
Hopfengardner. Cashman, Erin R.
United States. Office of
Educational Research and
Improvement.
Description: 33 p.; 28 cm.
Notes: Shipping list no.: 99-0149-
P. "February 1999"--T.p. verso.
Includes bibliographical
references (p. 17-33).
Subjects: Charter schools--United
States. Students with disabilities--
Education--United States.
LC Classification: LB2806.36
.F525 1999
Govt. Doc. No.: ED 1.302:C 38/3

Fiore, Thomas A.
Review of charter school
legislation provisions related to
students with disabilities /
prepared for Office of Educational
Research and Improvement, U.S.
Department of Education,
Washington, D.C.; prepared by
Thomas A. Fiore, Erin R.
Cashman.
Published/Created: Washington,
DC: The Office, [1999]
Related Authors: Cashman, Erin
R. United States. Office of
Educational Research and
Improvement.
Description: 44 p.; 28 cm.
Subjects: Charter schools--Law
and legislation--United States.
Handicapped children--
Education--Law and legislation
United States--States.
LC Classification: KF4129.Z95
F56 1999

Dewey Class No.: 371.01 21

Fitzgerald, Joy.
The state of charter schools in
Colorado: 1999-2000: the
characteristics, status and
performance record of Colorado
charter schools / Joy Fitzgerald;
[for the] Colorado Department of
Education.
Published/Created: Denver, CO:
The Department, [2001]
Related Authors: Colorado. Dept.
of Education.
Description: ix, 218 p.: ill.; 28
cm.
Notes: Title from cover. "March
2001." Includes statistics.
Includes bibliographical
references.
Subjects: Charter schools--
Colorado--Evaluation.
LC Classification: LB2806.36
.F529 2001
Dewey Class No.: 371.01 21

Florida. Legislature. Senate.
Committee on Education.
Charter schools and innovative
techniques / prepared for the
Florida Senate by staff of the
Committee on Education.
Published/Created: [Tallahassee]:
The Committee, [1996]
Related Authors: Florida.
Legislature. Senate.
Description: 23, A-3 p.; 28 cm.
Notes: "December 1996."
Subjects: Charter schools--
Florida. Education--Florida--
Experimental methods.
LC Classification: LB2806.36

.F56 1996
Dewey Class No.: 371.04 21

Florida. Office of Program Policy
Analysis and Government
Accountability.
OPPAGA program review:
charter schools need improved
academic accountability and
financial management / Office of
Program Policy Analysis and
Government Accountability.
Published/Created: Tallahassee,
FL (111 W. Madison St.,
Tallahassee 32399-1475): The
Office, 2000.
Description: i, 35 p.: 1 map; 28
cm.
Notes: Accompanied by review
summary. Cover title. "April
2000." Additional Form Avail.:
Also available on Worldwide
Web.
Subjects: Charter schools--
Florida--Evaluation. Educational
accountability--Florida.
Series: Report (Florida. Office of
Program Policy Analysis and
Government Accountability); no.
99-48.
Variant Series: Report; no. 99-48
LC Classification: LB2806.36
.F58 2000
Govt. Doc. No.: AUD.B 3:R
38/99-48 fldocs

Good, Thomas L., 1943-
The great school debate: choice,
vouchers, and charters / Thomas
L. Good, Jennifer S. Braden.
Published/Created: Mahwah, N.J.:
L. Erlbaum Associates, 2000.
Related Authors: Braden, Jennifer
S.
Description: xvii, 273 24 cm.
ISBN: 0805836918 (cloth: acid-
free paper) 0805835512 (paper:
acid-free paper)
Notes: Includes bibliographical
references and indexes.
Subjects: Privatization in
education--United States. School
choice--United States.
Educational vouchers--United
States. Charter schools--United
States. Education--United States--
Evaluation.
LC Classification: LB2806.36
.G66 2000
Dewey Class No.: 379.3/2/0973
21

Guidebook to Colorado charter
schools: key issues for start-up
and implementation of charter
schools / prepared by Carolyn G.
DeRaad, editor, for the Colorado
Children's Campaign, for the
Colorado Department of
Education.
Published/Created: Denver, Colo.:
Colorado State Board of
Education, [1997]
Related Authors: DeRaad,
Carolyn G. Colorado Children's
Campaign. Colorado. Dept. of
Education.
Description: 1 v. (various
pagings); 30 cm.
Notes: Cover title. "August 1997."
Includes bibliographical
references.

Subjects: Charter schools--
Colorado--Handbooks, manuals,
etc. School management and
organization--Colorado--
Handbooks, manuals, etc.
LC Classification: LB2806.36
.G85 1997
Dewey Class No.: 371.01 21

Hassel, Bryan C.
The charter school challenge:
avoiding the pitfalls, fulfilling the
promise / Bryan C. Hassel.
Published/Created: Washington,
D.C.: Brookings Institution Press,
c1999.
Description: viii, 193 p.: ill.; 24
cm. ISBN: 081573512X (cloth:
alk. paper) 0815735111 (pbk.:
alk. paper)
Notes: Includes bibliographical
references (p. 165-185) and index.
Subjects: Charter schools--United
States. Charter schools--Political
aspects--United States.
LC Classification: LB2806.36
.H37 1999
Dewey Class No.: 371.01 21

Hawaii. Legislature. Office of the
Legislative Auditor.
Allocation to new century charter
schools project, FY 2000-01: a
report to the Governor and the
Legislature of the State of Hawaii
/ submitted by the Auditor, State
of Hawaii.
Published/Created: Honolulu: The
Auditor, [2001]
Description: vi, 35 p.; 28 cm.
Notes: "January 2001." Overview
tipped in.

Subjects: Charter schools--
Hawaii--Finance. Educational law
and legislation--Hawaii.
Series: Report (Hawaii.
Legislature. Office of the
Legislative Auditor); no. 01-01.
Variant Series: Report no.; 01-01
LC Classification: LB2806.36
.H39 2001

Hirsch, Eric, 1970-
Colorado charter schools: a
comparison of charter and school
district spending / by Eric Hirsch,
Amy Berk Anderson.
Published/Created: Denver:
National Conference of State
Legislatures, c1999.
Related Authors: Anderson, Amy
Berk. National Conference of
State Legislatures.
Description: vii, 24 p.: ill.; 28
cm. ISBN: 1580240372
Notes: "October 1999." "Item
#3140"--Back cover. Includes
bibliographical references (p. 23-
24).
Subjects: Charter schools--
Colorado--Finance. Education--
Colorado--Finance.
LC Classification: LB2806.36
.H57 1999

How North Carolina became an
English colony (Filmstrip)
Published/Created: ELM
Historical Films, 1956.
Related Authors: Newsome,
Albert Ray, 1894-1951. The
growth of North Carolina.ELM
Historical Films, inc., Chapel
Hill, N.C.

Description: 58 fr., b&w, 35 mm.
Summary: Photographs of engravings, official documents, and paintings portray the responsibilities of the eight Lords Proprietor to whom Charles II issued the Carolina charter, the growth of settlements in North Carolina, the escapades of the pirate Edward Teach and other pirates who operated along the Carolina coast, and the activities of the Moravians, Scots, Quakers, and other groups who were among the early settlers. Includes pictures of early homes, churches, and schools which reflect the way of life during the 17th and 18th centuries.
Notes: With guide. Correlated with the textbook The growth of North Carolina, by A. R. Newsome and Hugh T. Lefler.
Subjects: North Carolina--History--Colonial period, ca. 1600-1775. North Carolina--Social life and customs.
Series: Historic North Carolina (Filmstrip) unit 2.
Variant Series: Historic North Carolina, unit 2

Illinois State Board of Education (1973-)
Annual report on Illinois charter schools / Illinois State Board of Education.
Published/Created: Springfield, Ill.: Illinois State Board of Education,
Description: v.; 28 cm.

Current Frequency: Annual
Continues: Illinois State Board of Education (1973-). Report on charter schools
(OCoLC)39245773
Notes: Title from caption. "This report is submitted in compliance with Section 27A-12 of the Illinois Charter Schools Law (105 ILCS 5/27A-12)." Description based on: 1999.
Subjects: Charter schools--Illinois. Charter schools--Law and legislation--Illinois.
LC Classification: IN PROCESS

Innovation & Massachusetts charter schools: a report / by Rosenblum Brigham Associates for the Massachusetts Department of Education.
Published/Created: [Malden, Mass.]: The Department, [1998]
Related Authors: Massachusetts. Dept. of Education.
Description: 32 p.; 28 cm.
Notes: Title from cover. "July, 1998." Includes bibliographical references (p. 31).
Subjects: Charter schools--Massachusetts. Educational innovations--Massachusetts.
LC Classification: LB2806.36 .I56 1998

Inside charter schools: the paradox of radical decentralization / edited by Bruce Fuller.
Published/Created: Cambridge, Mass.: Harvard University Press, 2000.

Related Authors: Fuller, Bruce.
Description: xiii, 285 p.; 25 cm.
ISBN: 067400325X (alk. paper)
Notes: Includes bibliographical
references (p. 257-273) and index.
Subjects: Charter schools--United
States. Schools--Decentralization-
-United States. Education and
state--United States.
LC Classification: LB2806.36
.I57 2000
Dewey Class No.: 371.01 21

Interdistrict magnet schools and
  charter schools report.
  Published/Created: [Hartford,
  Conn.]: State of Connecticut,
  State Board of Education, [1999]
  Related Authors: Connecticut.
  State Board of Education.
  Description: vii, 132 p.: col.
  maps; 28 cm.
  Notes: Title from cover. "Pursuant
  to Section 17 of Public Act 97-
  290 ..."--P. iv. "December 1998."
  Subjects: Educational
  equalization--Connecticut.
  Charter schools--Connecticut.
  Magnet schools--Connecticut.
  LC Classification: LB2806.36
  .I58 1999

Kowalski, Frank, 1907-1974.
  Papers of Frank Kowalski, 1925-
  1976 (bulk 1948-1963)
  Related Authors: Kowalski,
  Frank, 1907-1974. Niho Saisumbi
  (1969)
  Description: 7,500 items. 21
  containers plus 1 OV plus 1 CL.
  11 linear feet. Access Advisory:
  Restrictions apply. CLASSIFIED,

in part.
Biog./History Note: U.S. Army
officer and U.S. representative
from Connecticut.
Summary: Correspondence,
memoranda, writings, speeches,
reports, military orders, patents,
newspaper clippings, printed
materials, scrapbooks, drawings,
and photographs, pertaining
primarily to Kowalski's career in
the U.S. Army (1925-1958) and in
the U.S. House of Representatives
(1959-1963). Military files
document his directorship of the
Disarmament School, U.S. Army
Forces in the European Theater,
London, England (1944-1945)
and the school's training of Allied
and American officers for the
demobilization and disarmament
of Germany; his various
assignments during the U.S.
occupation of Japan (1948-1952),
particularly as chief of staff of the
American advisory group
overseeing the establishment of
the Japanese National Police
Reserve (Keisatsu Yobitai) at the
outbreak of the Korean War; and
his directorship of the Army
Command Management School,
Fort Belvoir, Va. (1954-1958).
Congressional files document his
work relating to several labor
disputes in Connecticut, his
interest in military reform as a
member of the House Committee
on Armed Services and its Special
Subcommittee on the Utilization
of Military Manpower, and his
opposition to the Vietnam War.

Postcongressional files relate to his membership on the Subversive Activities Control Board (1963-1966). Includes mss. describing the economic, political, and social conditions in Poland (1945); a report (1944) based on interviews of Polish-born soldiers who served in the German army; and fragments of Kowalski's ms. examining U.S. occupation and rearmament of Japan titled, Grace of Heaven, and published as Niho Saisumbi (Tokyo, 1969); and an unpublished ms. titled, Worms in Charter Oak, concerning Kowalski's political career and his relations with the Democratic state chairman of Connecticut, John M. Bailey. Correspondents include Bunzïo Akama, William Benton, Chester Bowles, Wilber Marion Brucker, Arleigh A. Burke, Chester R. Davis, Keizo Hayashi, Nishioka Hirokichi, William B. Huie, Robert F. Kennedy, Hiroo Konda, Keikichi Masuhara, Wilbur D. Mills, Adam Clayton Powell, Abraham Ribicoff, Sam Rayburn, Yoshizo Takeda, and Maxwell D. Taylor. Notes: MSS79561 Finding Aids: Finding aid available in the Manuscript Reading Room. Source of Acquisition: Gift, Barry Kowalski, 1990. Gift, Richard Lowitt, 1992. Subjects: Akama, Bunzïo, b. 1898. Bailey, John M. (John Moran), 1904-1975. Benton, William, 1900-1973. Bowles, Chester, 1901- Brucker, Wilber Marion, 1894-1968. Burke, Arleigh A., 1901- Davis, Chester R., 1896-1966. Hayashi, Keizo, 1907- Hirokichi, Nishioka. Huie, William Bradford, 1910-1986. Kennedy, Robert F., 1925-1968. Konda, Hiroo. Masuhara, Keikichi, b. 1903. Mills, Wilbur D. (Wilbur Daigh), 1909- Powell, Adam Clayton, 1908-1972. Ribicoff, Abraham, 1910- Rayburn, Sam, 1882-1961. Takeda, Yoshizïo, b. 1885. Taylor, Maxwell D. (Maxwell Davenport), 1901-1987. Japan. Keisatsu Yobitai. United States. Army--Management. United States. Army--Officers. United States. Army. Forces in the European Theater. Disarmament School. United States. Congress. House. United States. Congress. House. Committee on Armed Services. United States. Congress. House. Committee on Armed Services. Special Subcommittee on the Utilization of Manpower in the Military. United States. Subversive Activities Control Board. United States Army Command Management School. Labor disputes--Connecticut. Manpower planning--United States. Military government--Japan. Vietnamese Conflict, 1961-1975--Protest movements--United States. World War, 1939-1945--Personal narratives, Polish. Connecticut--Politics and government. Fort Belvoir (Va.)

Germany--Armed Forces--
Demobilization. Japan--Defenses.
Japan--History--Allied
occupation, 1945-1952. Japan--
Relations--United States. Poland--
Economic conditions--1945-1980.
Poland--Politics and government--
1945-1980. Poland--Social
conditions--1945- United States--
Foreign relations--1945- United
States--Politics and government--
1945- United States--Relations--
Japan. Army officers.
Representatives, U.S. Congress--
Connecticut.

La escuela protagonista: una propuesta
para dotar de autonomнa a las
escuelas / Blanco Etchegaray,
Agustina ... [et al.].
Edition Information: 1o [sic] ed.
Published/Created: Buenos Aires,
Argentina: Temas Grupo
Editorial, 1999.
Related Authors: Blanco
Etchegaray, Agustina. Grupo
Sophia.
Description: 235 p.: ill.; 23 cm.
ISBN: 9879164342
Notes: At foot of t.p.: Fundaciyn
Grupo Sophia. Includes
bibliographical references (p. 227-
235).
Subjects: Schools--
Decentralization--Argentina.
School autonomy--Argentina.
Charter schools--Argentina.
Series: Ensayo (Temas Grupo
Editorial (Buenos Aires,
Argentina)
Variant Series: Ensayo
LC Classification: LB2862 .E83

1999

Learning from school choice / Paul E.
Peterson, Bryan C. Hassel,
editors.
Published/Created: Washington,
D.C.: Brookings Institution Press,
c1998.
Related Authors: Peterson, Paul
E. Hassel, Bryan C.
Description: xii, 442 p.: ill.; 24
cm. ISBN: 0815770162 (cloth:
alk. paper) 0815770154 (pbk.:
alk. paper)
Contents: School choice: a report
card / Paul E. Peterson -- The case
for charter schools / Bryan C.
Hassel -- Governance and
educational quality / John E.
Brandl -- Civic values in public
and private schools / Jay P.
Greene -- Policy churn and the
plight of urban school reform /
Frederick M. Hess -- Analyzing
school choice reforms that use
America's traditional forms of
parental choice / Caroline M.
Hoxby -- Interdistrict choice in
Massachusetts / David L. Armour
and Brett M. Peiser -- Charter
schools as seen by students,
teachers, and parents / Gregg
Vanourek ... [et al.] -- The
performance of privately managed
schools: an early look at the
Edison Project / John E. Chubb --
Charter schools: politics and
practice in four states / Bryan C.
Hassel -- Comparing public
choice and private voucher
programs in San Antonio / R.
Kenneth Godwin, Frank R.

Kemerer, and Valerie J. Martinez
-- Evidence from the Indianapolis
voucher program / David J.
Weinschrott and Sally B. Kilgore
-- School choice in Milwaukee: a
randomized experiment / Jay P.
Greene, Paul E. Peterson, and
Jiangtao Du -- Lessons from the
Cleveland scholarship program /
Jay P. Greene, William Howell,
and Paul E. Peterson -- Why
parents should choose / Stephen
G. Gilles -- School choice and
state constitutional law / Joseph P.
Viteritti.
Notes: Includes bibliographical
references and index.
Subjects: Educational vouchers--
United States--Case studies.
School choice--United States--
Case studies. Charter schools--
United States--Case studies.
LC Classification: LB2828.8 .L43
1998
Dewey Class No.: 379.1/11/0973
21

Leonard-Osterwalder, Christine.
Charter schools / Christine
Leonard-Osterwalder.
Published/Created: Westminster,
Calif.: Teacher Created Materials,
c2000.
Description: vi, 74 p.: ill.; 23 cm.
ISBN: 1576904792
Notes: Includes bibliographical
references (p. 73-74).
Subjects: Charter schools--United
States.
Series: Professional's guide
LC Classification: LB2806.36

.L46 2000
Dewey Class No.: 371.01 21

Madsen, Jean.
Private and public school
partnerships: sharing lessons
about decentralization / Jean
Madsen.
Published/Created: London;
Washington, D.C.: Falmer Press,
1996.
Description: xv, 243 p.: ill.; 24
cm. ISBN: 0750705361 (cloth:
acid-free paper) Cancelled ISBN:
0750705374 (pbk.: acid-free
paper)
Notes: Includes bibliographical
references (p. 227-236) and index.
Subjects: Privatization in
education--United States--Case
studies. Charter schools--United
States--Case studies. Schools--
Decentralization--United States--
Case studies. Elementary school
administration--United States--
Case studies. Public schools--
United States--Case studies.
LC Classification: LB2806.36
.M25 1996
Dewey Class No.: 379.3/0973 20

Massachusetts. Office of the Inspector
General.
A management review of
Commonwealth charter schools /
Office of the Inspector General,
Commonwealth of Massachusetts.
Published/Created: [Boston]: The
Office, [1999]
Related Authors: Cerasoli, Robert
A.

Description: xviii, 144 p.; 28 cm.
Notes: Title from cover. "Robert
A. Cerasoli, Inspector General."
"November 1999." Includes
bibliographical references.
Subjects: Charter schools--
Massachusetts. School
management and organization--
Massachusetts.
LC Classification: LB2806.36
.M28 1999
Dewey Class No.: 371.01 21

Michigan's charter school initiative:
    from theory to practice / prepared
    for Michigan Department of
    Education; prepared by Public
    Sector Consultants, Inc.,
    Maximus, Inc.
    Published/Created: [Michigan?:
    s.n., 1999]
    Related Authors: Public Sector
    Consultants, Inc. Maximus, Inc.
    Description: 132, 8, 4, 15 p.: ill.;
    28 cm.
    Notes: Cover title. "January
    1999." Includes bibliographical
    references (p. 94-97).
    Subjects: Charter schools--
    Michigan. Education--Michigan.
    LC Classification: LB2806.36
    .M53 1999

Miron, Gary.
    Autonomy in exchange for
    accountability: an initial study of
    Pennsylvania charter schools /
    Gary Miron and Christopher
    Nelson.
    Published/Created: [Kalamazoo,
    Mich.]: Evaluation Center,
    Western Michigan University,

[2000]
Related Authors: Nelson,
Christopher. Pennsylvania. Dept.
of Education.
Description: 1 v. (various
pagings): ill. (some col.), maps;
28 cm.
Notes: Cover title. "October
2000." "... pursuant to a contract
with the Pennsylvania Department
of Education"--P. i. Includes
bibliographical references.
Subjects: Charter schools--
Pennsylvania. Educational
accountability--Pennsylvania.
LC Classification: LB2806.36
.M57 2000

Miron, Gary.
    What's public about charter
    schools?: lessons learned about
    choice and accountability / by
    Gary Miron and Christopher
    Nelson.
    Published/Created: Thousand
    Oaks, CA: Corwin Press, c2002.
    Projected Pub. Date: 0203
    Related Authors: Nelson,
    Christopher.
    Description: p. cm. ISBN:
    0761945377
    Notes: Includes bibliographical
    references and index.
    Subjects: Charter schools--
    Michigan--Evaluation.
    Educational accountability--
    Michigan. School choice--
    Michigan.
    LC Classification: LB2806.36
    .M58 2002
    Dewey Class No.: 371.01 21

Mulholland, Lori A.
Arizona charter school progress
evaluation / prepared by Lori A.
Mulholland for the Arizona
Department of Education.
Published/Created: Tempe, Ariz.
(PO Box 874405, Tempe 85287-
4405): Morrison Institute for
Public Policy, School of Public
Affairs, College of Public
Programs, Arizona State
University, [1999]
Related Authors: Morrison
Institute for Public Policy.
Arizona. Dept. of Education.
Description: 1 v. (various
pagings): ill.; 28 cm.
Notes: "March 1999."
Subjects: Charter schools--
Arizona. Public schools--Arizona.
Education--Arizona.
LC Classification: LB2806.36
.M84 1999
Govt. Doc. No.: ASU 12.2:C
41/999 azdocs

Murphy, Joseph, 1949-
Understanding and assessing the
charter school movement / Joseph
Murphy, Catherine Dunn
Shiffman.
Published/Created: New York:
Teachers College Press, 2002.
Projected Pub. Date: 0201
Related Authors: Shiffman,
Catherine Dunn.
Description: p. cm. ISBN:
080774199X (cloth: alk. paper)
0807741981 (pbk.: alk. paper)
Notes: Includes bibliographical
references and index.

Subjects: Charter schools--United
States. Educational change--
United States.
Series: Critical issues in
educational leadership series
LC Classification: LB2806.36
.M87 2002
Dewey Class No.: 371.01 21

Nathan, Joe, 1948-
Charter schools: creating hope
and opportunity for American
education / Joe Nathan.
Edition Information: 1st pbk. ed.
Published/Created: San Francisco:
Jossey-Bass Publishers, 1999.
Description: xxxiv, 254 p.; 23
cm. ISBN: 0787944548
Notes: Includes bibliographical
references (p. 227-238) and index.
Subjects: Charter schools--United
States.
Series: The Jossey-Bass education
series
LC Classification: LB2806.36
.N38 1999

Nathan, Joe, 1948-
Charter schools: creating hope
and opportunity for American
education / Joe Nathan.
Edition Information: 1st ed.
Published/Created: San Francisco:
Jossey-Bass Publishers, c1996.
Description: xx, 249 p.; 24 cm.
ISBN: 0787902632 (alk. paper)
Contents: Introduction: a new
choice -- Introducing charter
schools -- A tour of charter
schools -- The birth of a
movement -- How charter schools

are changing the system -- Breaking the district monopoly -- A new role for unions -- Creating charter schools -- Getting started -- Building support -- Staying in business -- Where to, what next -- Key early lessons -- Charting the future.
Notes: Includes bibliographical references (p. 223-233) and index.
Subjects: Charter schools--United States.
Series: The Jossey-Bass education series
LC Classification: LB2806.36 .N38 1996
Dewey Class No.: 371 20

National Urban League affiliate education accreditation guide / developed by education leadership consultants for National Urban League, Affiliate Development Department, CBO Partnership Program.
Published/Created: [New York?]: The League, c1996-
Related Authors: National Urban League. CBO Partnership Program.
Description: v. <1; 28 cm.
Incomplete
Contents: v. 1. Education accreditation: the basic processes for public schools, alternative schools, special schools and programs, charter schools
Notes: Cover title. "July 1996"-- T.p., v. 1.
Subjects: National Urban League. Public schools--Accreditation-- United States. Alternative

schools--Accreditation--United States. Charter schools-- Accreditation--United States.
LC Classification: LB2810.3 .N38 1996

Nehring, James.
Upstart startup: creating and sustaining a public charter school / James Nehring; foreword by Nancy and Theodore Sizer.
Published/Created: New York: Teachers College Press, c2002.
Description: xii, 180 p.; 24 cm.
ISBN: 0807741639 (cloth) 0807741620 (pbk.)
Notes: Includes bibliographical references (p. 9) and index.
Subjects: Charter schools--United States. School management and organization--United States.
LC Classification: LB2806.36 .N43 2002
Dewey Class No.: 371.01 21

Nelson, F. Howard.
Venturesome capital: state charter school finance systems / F. Howard Nelson, Edward Muir, Rachel Drown (American Federation of Teachers Educational Foundation).
Published/Created: [Washington, D.C.]: Office of Educational Research and Improvement, U.S. Dept. of Education; Jessup, MD: U.S. Dept. of Education, ED Pubs [distributor], [2000]
Related Authors: Muir, Edward. Drown, Rachel. American Federation of Teachers. Educational Foundation. National

Charter School Finance Study.
Description: vi, 185 p.; 28 cm.
Notes: "December 2000"--T.p.
verso. "GFI 2001-9501"--P. [4] of
cover. Includes bibliographical
references (p. 91-96).
Subjects: Charter schools--United
States--Finance.
LC Classification: LB2806.36
.N45 2000

New Jersey. Legislature. General
Assembly. Committee on
Education.
Public hearing before Assembly
Education Committee: the Charter
School Program Act of 1995: /
hearing recorded and transcribed
by the Office of Legislative
Services, Public Information
Office, Hearing Unit.
Published/Created: Trenton, N.J.
(State House Annex, PO 068,
Trenton): The Unit, [1998]
Description: [9] leaves, 151, 197
p.; 28 cm.
Notes: Cover title. "May 11,
1998."
Subjects: Charter schools--Law
and legislation--New Jersey.
Charter schools--New Jersey--
Evaluation.
LC Classification: KFN1811.4
.E35 1998

New Jersey. Legislature. Joint
Committee on the Public Schools.
Charter Schools Subcommittee.
Committee meeting of Joint
Committee on the Public Schools,
Charter Schools Subcommittee:

"to discuss the funding impact of
charter schools on school districts
in New Jersey" / meeting recorded
and transcribed by the Office of
Legislative Services, Public
Information Office, Hearing Unit.
Published/Created: Trenton, N.J.:
The Subcommittee, [1999]
Related Authors: New Jersey.
Office of Legislative Services.
Public Information Office.
Hearing Unit.
Description: 93, 66 p.; 28 cm.
Notes: Cover title. Meeting held
May 6, 1999, Trenton, N.J.
Subjects: Charter schools--New
Jersey--Finance. Education--New
Jersey--Finance. Charter schools--
New Jersey--Evaluation.
LC Classification: KFN1811
.P832 1999

New Jersey. Legislature. Senate.
Committee on Education.
Public hearing before Senate
Education Committee and
Assembly Education Committee:
charter schools / hearing
recordedand transcribed by the
Office of Legislative Services,
Public Information Office,
Hearing Unit.
Published/Created: Trenton, N.J.:
The Committee, [1995]
Related Authors: New Jersey.
Legislature. General Assembly.
Committee on Education.
Description: 88, 144 p.: ill.; 28
cm.
Notes: Cover title. Hearing held
December 5, 1995, Trenton, N.J.

Subjects: Charter schools--New Jersey. Educational change--New Jersey.
LC Classification: KFN1811.3 .E3 1995c

New Jersey. Legislature. Senate. Committee on Education.
Public hearing before Senate Education Committee: Senate bill no. 1796 (the Charter School Program Act of 1995) / hearing recorded and transcribed by the Office of Legislative Services, Public Information Office, Hearing Unit.
Published/Created: Trenton, N.J.: The Committee, [1995]
Description: 72, 26 p.; 28 cm.
Notes: Cover title. Hearing held Apr. 6, 1995, Rowan College, Glassboro, N.J.
Subjects: Charter schools--Law and legislation--New Jersey.
LC Classification: KFN1811.3 .E3 1995b

New Jersey. Legislature. Senate. Committee on Education.
Public hearing before Senate Education Committee: Senate bill no. 1796 (the Charter School Program Act of 1995) / hearing recorded and transcribed by the Office of Legislative Services, Public Information Office, Hearing Unit.
Published/Created: Trenton, N.J.: The Committee, [1995]
Description: 6, 81, 12 p.; 28 cm.
Notes: Cover title. Hearing held Apr. 28, 1995, Seminar Room,

A.J.J.A. Wilson Alumni Center, New Jersey Institute of Technology, Newark, N.J.
Subjects: Charter schools--Law and legislation--New Jersey.
LC Classification: KFN1811.3 .E3 1995e
Dewey Class No.: 344.749/071 21

Premack, Eric.
Charter school development guide / by Eric Premack.
Edition Information: California ed.
Published/Created: [California]: E. Premack, c1997.
Description: vi, 99 p.: forms; 28 cm.
Notes: Includes bibliographical references.
Subjects: Charter schools--California--Handbooks, manuals, etc.
LC Classification: LB2806.36 .P47 1997

Reconfiguring the structure of school districts.
Published/Created: [Carson City]: Legislative Counsel Bureau, [1997]
Related Authors: Nevada. Legislature. Legislative Counsel Bureau.
Description: vi, 424 p.: ill. (maps); 28 cm.
Notes: "January 1997." Includes bibliographical references.
Subjects: Education and state--Nevada. School districts--Nevada--Administration. Charter schools--Nevada. School districts--Nevada-

-Evaluation.
Series: Bulletin (Nevada.
Legislature. Legislative Counsel
Bureau); no. 97-4.
Variant Series: Bulletin; no. 97-4
LC Classification: LC90.N3 R43
1997
Dewey Class No.: 379.793 21

Rhetoric versus reality: what we know
and what we need to know about
vouchers and charter schools /
Brian P. Gill ... [et al.].
Published/Created: Santa Monica,
CA: Rand, 2001.
Projected Pub. Date: 0112
Related Authors: Gill, Brian P.,
1968-
Description: p. cm. ISBN:
0833027654
Notes: "MR-1118." Includes
bibliographical references.
Subjects: Educational vouchers.
Charter schools. School choice.
Educational vouchers--United
States. Charter schools--United
States. School choice--United
States.
LC Classification: LB2828.7 .R44
2001
Dewey Class No.: 379.1/11 21

SABIS International Charter School:
management issues and
recommendations / Office of the
Inspector General,
Commonwealth of Massachusetts.
Published/Created: Boston, MA:
The Office, 2000.
Related Authors: Massachusetts.
Office of the Inspector General.

Description: vi, 40, [7] p.; 28 cm.
Notes: Title from cover.
"November 2000." Includes
bibliographical references.
Additional Form Avail.: Also
available online; Adobe Acrobat
reader software required.
Subjects: SABIS International
Charter School (Springfield,
Mass.) Charter schools--
Massachusetts--Springfield--
Evaluation.
LC Classification: LB2806.36
.S23 2000

Sarason, Seymour Bernard, 1919-
Charter schools: another flawed
educational reform? / Seymour B.
Sarason.
Published/Created: New York:
Teachers College Press, c1998.
Description: viii, 115 p.; 23 cm.
ISBN: 0807737852 (cloth: alk.
paper) 0807737844 (paper: alk.
paper)
Notes: Includes bibliographical
references (p. 113-114).
Subjects: Charter schools--United
States. Education and state--
United States. Educational
change--United States.
Series: The series on school
reform
LC Classification: LB2806.36
.S27 1998
Dewey Class No.: 371.01 21

Sarason, Seymour Bernard, 1919-
Questions you should ask about
charter schools and vouchers /
Seymour B. Sarason.

Published/Created: Portsmouth, NH: Heinemann, c2002. Projected Pub. Date: 0202 Description: p. cm. ISBN: 0325004056 (alk. paper) Notes: Includes bibliographical references. Subjects: Charter schools--United States. Educational vouchers--United States. School choice--United States. LC Classification: LB2806.36 .S275 2002 Dewey Class No.: 379.1/11/0973 21

School choice in America: the great debate / Kim K. Metcalf, Patricia A. Muller, Natalie A. Legan, editors. Published/Created: Bloomington, Ind.: Phi Delta Kappa International, c2001. Related Authors: Metcalf, Kim K. Muller, Patricia A. Legan, Natalie A. Phi Delta Kappa. Center on Evaluation, Development, and Research. Description: 292 p.: ill.; 28 cm. Notes: On cover: Center for Evaluation, Development, Research, Phi Delta Kappa. "June 2001." Includes bibliographical references. Subjects: School choice--United States. Public schools--United States. Charter schools--United States. Private schools--United States. Educational vouchers--United States. Series: Hot topics series LC Classification: LB1027.9

.S3527 2001

School choice in the real world: lessons from Arizona charter schools / edited by Robert Maranto ... [et al.]. Published/Created: Boulder, Colo.: Westview Press, c2001. Related Authors: Maranto, Robert, 1958- Description: xiv, 271 p.; 22 cm. ISBN: 0813398207 Notes: Includes bibliographical references and index. Subjects: Charter schools--Arizona. School choice--Arizona. LC Classification: LB2806.36 .S3416 2001 Dewey Class No.: 379.1/11/09791 21

School choice in the real world: lessons from Arizona charter schools / edited by Robert Maranto ... [et al.]. Published/Created: Boulder, Colo.: Westview Press, c1999. Related Authors: Maranto, Robert, 1958- Description: xiv, 271 p.: ill., maps; 24 cm. ISBN: 0813366003 (alk. paper) Notes: Includes bibliographical references and index. Subjects: Charter schools--Arizona. School choice--Arizona. LC Classification: LB2806.36 .S3416 1999 Dewey Class No.: 379.1/11/09791 21

Schorr, Jonathan.
A school built on hope / Jonathan Schorr.
Published/Created: New York: Ballantine Books, 2002.
Projected Pub. Date: 0209
Description: p. cm. ISBN: 0345447026
Subjects: Charter schools--California--Oakland--Case studies. Educational equalization--California--Oakland--Case studies. Education, Urban--California--Oakland--Case studies.
LC Classification: LB2806.36 .S35 2002
Dewey Class No.: 371.01 21

Smith, Stacy, 1968-
The democratic potential of charter schools / Stacy Smith.
Published/Created: New York: P. Lang, c2001.
Description: 292 p.; 23 cm.
ISBN: 0820449091 (pbk.: alk. paper)
Notes: Includes bibliographical references (p. [271]-282) and index.
Subjects: Charter schools--United States--Case studies. School choice--Social aspects--United States--Case studies. Citizenship--Study and teaching--United States--Case studies. Educational equalization--United States--Case studies.
Series: Counterpoints (New York, N.Y.); v. 136.
Variant Series: Counterpoints,

1058-1634; v. 136
LC Classification: LB2806.36 .S65 2001
Dewey Class No.: 371.01 21

Test results from Massachusetts charter schools: a preliminary study.
Published/Created: Malden, Mass. (350 Main St., Malden 02148-5023): Massachusetts Dept. of Education, c1997.
Related Authors: Massachusetts. Dept. of Education.
Description: 55 p.; 28 cm.
Notes: "June, 1997." Title from cover.
Subjects: Charter schools--Massachusetts. School management and organization--Massachusetts. Educational tests and measurements--Massachusetts. Educational evaluation--Massachusetts.
LC Classification: LB2806.36 .T47 1997

Texas. Legislative Budget Board.
Charter schools: experiments in reform / prepared by Legislative Budget Board staff in cooperation with the Educational Economic Policy Center; presented to Legislative Budget Board [and] Educational Economic Policy Committee.
Published/Created: [Austin, Tex.]: The Board, [1994]
Description: 20 p.; 28 cm.
Notes: "June 1994." Includes bibliographical references (p. 19).

Subjects: School-based management--United States. School-based management--Texas. Charter schools--United States. Charter schools--Texas. School improvement programs--United States. School improvement programs--Texas. Educational change--United States. Educational change--Texas.
LC Classification: LB2806.35 .T49 1994
Dewey Class No.: 371.2/00973 20
Govt. Doc. No.: L1300.8 C385 txdocs

The charter school roadmap / Education Commission of the States, National Conference of State Legislatures.
Published/Created: Washington, DC: U.S. Dept. of Education, Office of Educational Research and Improvement: For sale by U.S. G.P.O., Supt. of Docs., [1998]
Related Authors: Education Commission of the States. National Conference of State Legislatures.
Description: vi, 69 p.; 28 cm.
ISBN: 0160497019
Notes: "September 1998"--T.p. verso. Includes bibliographical references (p. 69). Additional Form Avail.: Also available via Internet from the Department's home page at http://www.ed.gov.
Subjects: Charter schools--United States. School management and organization--United States.

Educational change--United States. School improvement programs--United States. Charter schools--Law and legislation--United States.
LC Classification: LB2806.36 .C53 1998

The Colorado charter schools evaluation / prepared for Colorado Department of Education by the Clayton Foundation and the Center for Human Investment Policy at the University of Colorado at Denver.
Published/Created: [Denver, Colo.]: Colorado Dept. of Education, [1997]
Related Authors: Colorado. Dept. of Education. Clayton Foundation for Research. University of Colorado at Denver. Center for Human Investment Policy.
Description: i, 79 p.: ill.; 28 cm.
Notes: Cover title. "March 1997." Includes statistics. Includes bibliographical references.
Subjects: Charter schools--Colorado--Evaluation.
LC Classification: LB2806.36 .C65 1997
Govt. Doc. No.: ED2.2/C38/1997 codocs

The state of charter schools 2000: fourth-year report / RPP International; Beryl Nelson ... [et al.].
Published/Created: Washington, DC: Office of Educational Research and Improvement, U.S. Dept. of Education: For sale by

the U.S. G.P.O., Supt. of Docs.,
[2000]
Related Authors: Nelson, Beryl.
RPP International.
Description: iv, 56 p.: ill.; 28 cm.
Notes: "January 2000"--T.p.
verso.
Subjects: Charter schools--United
States--Statistics.
LC Classification: LB2806.36
.S72 2000
Dewey Class No.: 371.01 21

The state of charter schools: third-year
report / RPP International; Paul
Berman ... [et al.].
Published/Created: Washington,
DC: Office of Educational
Research and Improvement, U.S.
Dept. of Education: For sale by
the U.S. G.P.O., Supt. of Docs.,
1999.
Related Authors: Berman, Paul,
1937- RPP International.
Description: vi, 56 p.: ill.; 28 cm.
ISBN: 0160500486
Notes: "SAI 1999-3010"--P. [4]
of cover.
Subjects: Charter schools--United
States--Statistics.
LC Classification: LB2806.36
.S72 1999

United States. Congress. House.
Committee on Economic and
Educational Opportunities.
Subcommittee on Oversight and
Investigations.
Hearings on DC school reform:
hearings before the Subcommittee
on Oversight and Investigations of

the Committee on Economic and
Educational Opportunities, House
of Representatives, One Hundred
Fourth Congress, first session,
hearings held in Washington, DC,
June 8 and 27, 1995.
Published/Created: Washington:
U.S. G.P.O.: For sale by the U.S.
G.P.O., Supt. of Docs.,
Congressional Sales Office, 1995
[i.e. 1996]
Description: iv, 261 p.; 24 cm.
ISBN: 0160528437
Notes: Distributed to some
depository libraries in microfiche.
Shipping list no.: 96-0306-P.
"Serial no. 104-52." Includes
bibliographical references.
Subjects: Public Schools of the
District of Columbia. School
management and organization--
Washington (D.C.) Charter
schools--Washington (D.C.)
Educational vouchers--
Washington (D.C.) School
improvement programs--
Washington (D.C.) Educational
change--Washington (D.C.)
LC Classification: KF27 .E367
1995n
Dewey Class No.: 371.01/09753
21
Govt. Doc. No.: Y 4.ED 8/1:104-
52

United States. Congress. House.
Committee on Education and the
Workforce.
The success of charter schools:
hearing before the Committee on
Education and the Workforce,

House of Representatives, One Hundred Sixth Congress, second session, hearing held in Washington, DC, September 28, 2000.
Published/Created: Washington: U.S. G.P.O.: [U.S. G.P.O., Supt. of Docs., Congressional Sales Office, distributor], 2000.
Description: iv, 168 p.: ill.; 24 cm. ISBN: 0160644860
Notes: Distributed to some depository libraries in microfiche.
Shipping list no.: 2001-0068-P.
"Serial no. 106-129." Includes bibliographical references and index.
Subjects: Charter schools--United States.
LC Classification: KF27 .E3+
Govt. Doc. No.: Y 4.ED 8/1:106-129

United States. Congress. House. Committee on Education and the Workforce. Subcommittee on Early Childhood, Youth, and Families.
Charter schools: hearing before the Subcommittee on Early Childhood, Youth, and Families of the Committee on Education and the Workforce, House of Representatives, One Hundred Fifth Congress, first session, hearing held in Washington, DC, June 26, 1997.
Published/Created: Washington: U.S. G.P.O.: For sale by the U.S. G.P.O., Supt. of Docs., Congressional Sales Office, 1998.
Description: iv, 211 p.: ill.; 24

cm. ISBN: 0160573742
Notes: Distributed to some depository libraries in microfiche.
Shipping list no.: 98-0351-P.
"Serial no. 105-136."
Subjects: Charter schools--United States. Educational change--United States.
LC Classification: KF27 .E3328 1997h
Dewey Class No.: 371.01 21
Govt. Doc. No.: Y 4.ED 8/1:105-136

United States. Congress. House. Committee on Education and the Workforce. Subcommittee on Early Childhood, Youth, and Families.
Charter schools: hearing before the Subcommittee on Early Childhood, Youth, and Families of the Committee on Education and the Workforce, House of Representatives, One Hundred Fifth Congress, first session, hearing held in Washington, DC, September 16, 1997.
Published/Created: Washington: U.S. G.P.O.: For sale by the U.S. G.P.O., Supt. of Docs., Congressional Sales Office, 1998.
Description: iv, 156 p.: ill., map; 24 cm. ISBN: 016057403X
Notes: Distributed to some depository libraries in microfiche.
Shipping list no.: 98-0363-P.
"Serial no. 105-141." Includes bibliographical references.
Subjects: Charter schools--United States. Education and state--United States. Educational

change--United States.
LC Classification: KF27 .E3328
1997m
Dewey Class No.: 371.01 21
Govt. Doc. No.: Y 4.ED 8/1:105-
141

United States. Congress. House.
Committee on Education and the
Workforce. Subcommittee on
Early Childhood, Youth, and
Families.
Excellence in education through
innovative alternatives: hearing
before the Subcommittee on Early
Childhood, Youth, and Families
of the Committee on Education
and the Workforce, House of
Representatives, One Hundred
Sixth Congress, first session,
hearing held in Greenville, South
Carolina, August 12, 1999.
Published/Created: Washington:
U.S. G.P.O.: For sale by the U.S.
G.P.O., Supt. of Docs.,
Congressional Sales Office, 2000.
Description: iii, 93 p.: ill.; 24 cm.
ISBN: 0160601258
Notes: Distributed to some
depository libraries in microfiche.
Shipping list no.: 2000-0166-P.
Includes index. "Serial no. 106-
66."
Subjects: Educational
innovations--South Carolina--
Greenville. Total quality
management in education--South
Carolina Greenville. Charter
schools--South Carolina--
Greenville. Magnet schools--
South Carolina--Greenville.

LC Classification: KF27 .E3328
1999+
Govt. Doc. No.: Y 4.ED 8/1:106-
66

United States. Congress. House.
Committee on Education and the
Workforce. Subcommittee on
Early Childhood, Youth, and
Families.
Private and public school choice:
hearing before the Subcommittee
on Early Childhood, Youth, and
Families of the Committee on
Education and the Workforce,
House of Representatives, One
Hundred Fifth Congress, first
session, hearing held in
Washington, DC, September 30,
1997.
Published/Created: Washington:
U.S. G.P.O.: For sale by the U.S.
G.P.O., Supt. of Docs.,
Congressional Sales Office, 1998.
Description: iv, 168 p.: ill.; 24
cm. ISBN: 0160573505
Notes: Distributed to some
depository libraries in microfiche.
Shipping list no.: 98-0350-P.
Includes index. "Serial no. 105-
135."
Subjects: School choice--United
States. Educational vouchers--
United States. Charter schools--
United States. Privatization in
education--United States.
LC Classification: KF27 .E3328
1997p
Dewey Class No.: 379.1/11 21
Govt. Doc. No.: Y 4.ED 8/1:105-

135

United States. Congress. House. Committee on Education and the Workforce. Subcommittee on Oversight and Investigations. Charter schools: successes and challenges: hearing before the Subcommittee on Oversight and Investigations of the Committee on Education and the Workforce, House of Representatives, One Hundred Sixth Congress, second session, hearing held in Washington, DC, March 3, 2000. Published/Created: Washington: U.S. G.P.O.: For sale by the U.S. G.P.O., Supt. of Docs., Congressional Sales Office, 2000. Description: iii, 97 p.; 24 cm. ISBN: 0160607051 Notes: Distributed to some depository libraries in microfiche. Shipping list no.: 2000-0319-P. Includes index. "Serial no. 106-91." Subjects: Charter schools--United States. LC Classification: KF27 .E367+ Govt. Doc. No.: Y 4.ED 8/1:106-91

United States. Congress. House. Committee on Education and the Workforce. Subcommittee on Oversight and Investigations. Education at a crossroads: what works and what's wasted?: hearings before the Subcommittee on Oversight and Investigations of the Committee on Education and the Workforce, House of Representatives, One Hundred Fifth Congress, first session, hearings held in Napa, California, San Fernando, California, January 29, 30, and Phoenix, Arizona, January 31, 1997. Published/Created: Washington: U.S. G.P.O.: For sale by the U.S. G.P.O., Supt. of Docs., Congressional Sales Office, 1997. Description: v, 632 p.: ill; 24 cm. ISBN: 0160551080 Notes: Distributed to some depository libraries in microfiche. Shipping list no.: 97-0280-P. "Serial no. 105-11." Includes bibliographical references. Subjects: Educational change--California. Educational change--Arizona. Federal aid to education--California. Federal aid to education--Arizona. Educational innovations--California. Educational innovations--Arizona. Charter schools--California. Charter schools--Arizona. LC Classification: KF27 .E367 1997f Dewey Class No.: 379.1/5/0973 21 Govt. Doc. No.: Y 4.ED 8/1:105-11

United States. Congress. House. Committee on Education and the Workforce. Subcommittee on Oversight and Investigations. Putting performance first: academic accountability and school choice in Florida: hearing before the Subcommittee on Oversight and Investigations of the Committee on Education and the Workforce, House of Representatives, One Hundred Sixth Congress, second session, hearing held in Temple Terrace, Florida, March 27, 2000. Published/Created: Washington: U.S. G.P.O.: For sale by the U.S. G.P.O., Supt. of Docs., Congressional Sales Office, 2000. Description: iv, 331 p.: ill.; 24 cm. ISBN: 016060740X Notes: Distributed to some depository libraries in microfiche. Shipping list no.: 2000-0312-P. Includes index. "Serial no. 106-100." Subjects: Educational accountability--Florida. School choice--Florida. Charter schools--Florida. School improvement programs--Florida. LC Classification: KF27 .E367+ Govt. Doc. No.: Y 4.ED 8/1:106-100

United States. Congress. House. Committee on the Judiciary. Subcommittee on the Constitution. Civil Rights Division of the U.S. Department of Justice regarding charter schools: hearing before the Subcommittee on the Constitution of the Committee on the Judiciary, House of Representatives, One Hundred Sixth Congress, first session, October 14, 1999. Published/Created: Washington: U.S. G.P.O.: For sale by the U.S.

G.P.O., Supt. of Docs., Congressional Sales Office, 2000. Description: iii, 177 p.: ill.; 24 cm. ISBN: 0160611393 Notes: Distributed to depository libraries in microfiche. Shipping list no.: 2001-0020-P. "Serial no. 80." Includes bibliographical references. Subjects: United States. Dept. of Justice. Civil Rights Division. Charter schools--United States. LC Classification: KF27 .J8565+ Govt. Doc. No.: Y 4.J 89/1:106/80

United States. Congress. Senate. Committee on Appropriations. Subcommittee on Departments of Labor, Health and Human Services, Education, and Related Agencies. Charter schools: hearing before a subcommittee of the Committee on Appropriations, United States Senate, One Hundred Fourth Congress, first session, special hearing. Published/Created: Washington: U.S. G.P.O.: For sale by the U.S. G.P.O., Supt. of Docs., Congressional Sales Office, 1995. Description: iii, 78 p.: ill.; 24 cm. ISBN: 0160470579 Notes: "Printed for the use of the Committee on Appropriations." Subjects: Charter schools--United States. School management and organization--United States. School improvement programs--United States.

Series: S. hrg.; 104-16
LC Classification: KF26 .A653
1995m
Dewey Class No.: 371/.04 20

United States. Congress. Senate.
Committee on Governmental
Affairs. Subcommittee on
Oversight of Government
Management, Restructuring, and
the District of Columbia.
Improvement opportunities for the
public schools in the District of
Columbia: hearing before the
Subcommittee on Oversight of
Government Management,
Restructuring, and the District of
Columbia of the Committee on
Governmental Affairs, United
States Senate, One Hundred Fifth
Congress, first session, April 17,
1997.
Published/Created: Washington:
U.S. G.P.O.: For sale by the U.S.
G.P.O., Supt. of Docs.,
Congressional Sales Office, 1998.
Description: iv, 275 p.: ill.; 24
cm. ISBN: 0160561086
Notes: Distributed to some
depository libraries in microfiche.
Shipping list no.: 98-0159-P.
Includes bibliographical
references.
Subjects: Public Schools of the
District of Columbia. School
management and organization--
Washington (D.C.) School
improvement programs--
Washington (D.C.) Charter
schools--Washington (D.C.)
Educational vouchers--
Washington (D.C.) Educational

change--Washington (D.C.)
Series: United States. Congress.
Senate. S. hrg.; 105-327.
Variant Series: S. hrg.; 105-327
LC Classification: KF26 .G6735
1997d
Dewey Class No.: 371.01/09753
21
Govt. Doc. No.: Y 4.G
74/9:S.HRG.105-327

United States. Congress. Senate.
Committee on Governmental
Affairs. Subcommittee on
Oversight of Government
Management, Restructuring, and
the District of Columbia.
Lessons learned in the D.C. public
schools: hearing before the
Subcommittee on Oversight of
Government Management,
Restructuring, and the District of
Columbia of the Committee on
Governmental Affairs, United
States Senate, One Hundred Fifth
Congress, second session, March
9, 1998.
Published/Created: Washington:
U.S. G.P.O.: For sale by the U.S.
G.P.O., Supt. of Docs.,
Congressional Sales Office, 1998.
Description: iii, 134 p.: ill.; 24
cm. ISBN: 0160571979
Notes: Distributed to some
depository libraries in microfiche.
Shipping list no.: 98-0336-P.
Includes bibliographical
references.
Subjects: Public Schools of the
District of Columbia. Public
schools--Washington (D.C.)
Federal aid to education--

Washington (D.C.) Educational change--Washington (D.C.) Charter schools--Washington (D.C.) Series: United States. Congress. Senate. S. hrg.; 105-537. Variant Series: S. hrg.; 105-537 LC Classification: KF26 .G6735 1998a Dewey Class No.: 371.01/09753 21 Govt. Doc. No.: Y 4.G 74/9:S.HRG.105-537

United States. Congress. Senate. Committee on Governmental Affairs. Subcommittee on Oversight of Government Management, Restructuring, and the District of Columbia. A progress report on the reforms in D.C. public schools: hearing before the Subcommittee on Oversight of Government Management, Restructuring, and the District of Columbia of the Committee on Governmental Affairs, United States Senate, One Hundred Fifth Congress, first session, September 8, 1997. Published/Created: Washington: U.S. G.P.O.: For sale by the U.S. G.P.O., Supt. of Docs., Congressional Sales Office, 1998. Description: iii, 101 p.: ill.; 24 cm. ISBN: 0160562309 Notes: Distributed to some depository libraries in microfiche. Shipping list no.: 98-0179-P. Includes bibliographical references.

Subjects: Public Schools of the District of Columbia-- Management. Public schools-- Washington (D.C.) Educational change--Washington (D.C.) Charter schools--Washington (D.C.) Educational vouchers-- Washington (D.C.) Series: United States. Congress. Senate. S. hrg.; 105-364. Variant Series: S. hrg.; 105-364 LC Classification: KF26 .G6735 1997j Govt. Doc. No.: Y 4.G 74/9:S.HRG.105-364

United States. Congress. Senate. Committee on Labor and Human Resources. Overview of charter schools: hearing of the Committee on Labor and Human Resources, United States Senate, One Hundred Fifth Congress, second session ... March 31, 1998. Published/Created: Washington: U.S. G.P.O.: For sale by the U.S. G.P.O., Supt. of Docs., Congressional Sales Office, 1998. Description: iii, 101 p.: ill.; 24 cm. ISBN: 016057045X Notes: Distributed to some depository libraries in microfiche. Shipping list no.: 98-0317-P. Includes bibliographical references (p. 90). Subjects: Charter schools--United States. Series: United States. Congress. Senate. S. hrg.; 105-483. Variant Series: S. hrg.; 105-483

LC Classification: KF26 .L27
1998o
Dewey Class No.: 371.01 21
Govt. Doc. No.: Y 4.L
11/4:S.HRG.105-483

United States. General Accounting
Office.
Charter schools: limited access to
facility financing: report to
Congressional requesters / United
States General Accounting Office.
Published/Created: Washington,
D.C. (P.O. Box 37050,
Washington 20013): The Office,
[2000]
Description: 28 p.: ill.; 28 cm.
Notes: Cover title. "September
2000." "GAO/HEHS-00-163."
"B-284442"--Letter of transmittal.
Includes bibliographical
references.
Subjects: Charter schools--United
States--Finance. School facilities-
-United States--Finance.
LC Classification: LB2806.36
.U53 2000
Dewey Class No.: 371.01 21

United States. General Accounting
Office.
Charter schools: new model for
public schools provides
opportunities and challenges:
report to Congressional requesters
/ United States General
Accounting Office.
Published/Created: Washington,
D.C.: The Office, [1995]
Description: 47 p.: ill.; 28 cm.
Notes: Cover title. "January
1995." "GAO/HEHS-95-42." "B-

256567"--P. 1. Includes
bibliographical references.
Subjects: School-based
management--United States.
Charter schools--United States.
Educational accountability--
United States. Education and
state--United States. Free schools-
-United States.
LC Classification: LB2806.35
.U55 1995b
Dewey Class No.: 371.2/00973 20
Govt. Doc. No.: GA 1.13:HEHS-
95-42

Urahn, Susan.
Minnesota charter schools: a
research report / [prepared by Sue
Urahn and Dan Stewart].
Published/Created: St. Paul, MN:
Research Dept., Minnesota House
of Representatives, [1994]
Related Authors: Stewart, Dan.
Minnesota. Legislature. House of
Representatives. Research Dept.
Description: 65 p.: ill.; 28 cm.
Notes: "December 1994."
Includes bibliographical
references (p. 65).
Subjects: School-based
management--Minnesota. Charter
schools--Minnesota.
LC Classification: LB2806.35
.U73 1994
Dewey Class No.: 371.2/00776 20

Vergari, Sandra.
The charter school landscape /
Sandra Vergari.
Published/Created: Pittsburgh,
Pa.: University of Pittsburgh
Press, c2002.

Projected Pub. Date: 0206
Description: p. cm. ISBN:
0822941805 (cloth: alk. paper)
Notes: Includes bibliographical
references (p.) and index.
Subjects: Charter schools--
Political aspects--United States.
LC Classification: LB2806.36
.V47 2002
Dewey Class No.: 371.01 21

Virginia. General Assembly. Joint
Subcommittee Studying Charter
Schools Pursuant to HJR 551 and
SJR 334.
Report of the Joint Subcommittee
Studying Charter Schools
Pursuant to HJR 551 and SJR 334
to the Governor and the General
Assembly of Virginia.
Published/Created: Richmond:
Commonwealth of Virginia, 1996.
Description: 1 v. (various
pagings): map; 28 cm.
Notes: Cover title. Includes
bibliographical references.
Subjects: Charter schools--
Virginia. School management and
organization--Virginia.
Series: House document
(Virginia. General Assembly.
House of Delegates); 1996, no.
43.
Variant Series: House document;
no. 43
LC Classification: J87 .V9 1996c
no. 43

Weil, Danny K., 1953-
Charter schools: a reference
handbook / Danny Weil.

Published/Created: Santa Barbara,
Calif.: ABC-CLIO, c2000.
Description: xi, 211 p.; 24 cm.
ISBN: 1576072452
Notes: Includes bibliographical
references and index.
Subjects: Charter schools--United
States.
Series: Contemporary education
issues
LC Classification: LB2806.36
.W45 2000
Dewey Class No.: 371.01/0973 21

Whitesel, Russ.
New law relating to charter
schools: 1993 Wisconsin Act 16 /
prepared by Russ Whitesel.
Published/Created: Madison, Wis.
(1 E. Main St., Suite 401,
Madison): Wisconsin Legislative
Council Staff, [1994]
Related Authors: Wisconsin.
Legislature. Legislative Council.
Description: 7 leaves; 28 cm.
Notes: Caption title. "June 23,
1994."
Subjects: Charter schools--Law
and legislation--Wisconsin.
Series: Information memorandum
(Wisconsin. Legislature.
Legislative Council: 1993); 94-
22.
Variant Series: Information
memorandum; 94-22
LC Classification: KFW2791.C57
W45 1994
Dewey Class No.: 344.775/073
347.750473 20
Govt. Doc. No.:

LEG.3:IM/1994/22 widocs

Wisconsin charter schools.
Published/Created: Madison,
Wis.: Wisconsin Dept. of Public
Instruction, [1997?-
Related Authors: Wisconsin.
Dept. of Public Instruction.
Description: v.: ill.; 28 cm.
1996/97-
Current Frequency: Annual
Notes: SERBIB/SERLOC merged
record
Subjects: Charter schools--
Wisconsin--Directories. Charter
schools--Wisconsin--Statistics--
Periodicals.
Series: Bulletin (Wisconsin. Dept.
of Public Instruction)
Variant Series: Bulletin
LC Classification: LB2806.36
.W57
Govt. Doc. No.: ED.6/2:C
45/1997- widocs

Wisconsin. Legislature. Legislative
Audit Bureau.
Charter School Program: an
evaluation / [prepared by Paul
Stuiber ... et al.].
Published/Created: Madison, WI:
Legislative Audit Bureau, [1998]
Related Authors: Stuiber, Paul.
Description: 62, I-37, [2], 2 p.:
maps; 28 cm.
Notes: "December 1998."
Subjects: Charter schools--
Wisconsin--Evaluation.
Privatization in education--
Wisconsin--Evaluation.
Series: Report (Wisconsin.
Legislature. Legislative Audit

Bureau); 98-15.
Variant Series: Report /
Wisconsin Legislative Audit
Bureau; 98-15
LC Classification: LB2806.36
.W58 1998
Dewey Class No.: 371.01 21
Govt. Doc. No.: AUD
2.3/2:1998/15 widocs

Wood, Jennifer, M.P.P.
An early examination of the
Massachusetts charter school
initiative / prepared by Jennifer
Wood (University of
Massachusetts, Donahue
Institute).
Published/Created: [Boston,
Mass.]: Massachusetts Education
Reform Review Commission,
[1999]
Related Authors: Donahue
Institute. Massachusetts
Education Reform Review
Commission.
Description: 1 v. (various
pagings); 28 cm.
Notes: "In 1997 the state
legislature charged MERRC
[Massachusetts Education reform
Review Commission] with
completing an independent
evaluation of the
Commonwealth's Charter School
Initiative. The research was
conducted under contract with the
University of Massachusetts
Donahue Institute. The findings
and recommendations contained
in the final report were endorsed
at the Commission's meeting on
December 6, 1999"--Letter of

transmittal. Title from cover.
Includes bibliographical
references. LC copy lacks letter of
transmittal.
Subjects: Charter schools--
Massachusetts--Evaluation.
LC Classification: LB2806.36
.W66 1999
Dewey Class No.: 371.01 21

Yancey, Patty, 1949-
Parents founding charter schools:
dilemmas of empowerment and
decentralization / Patty Yancey.
Published/Created: New York: P.
Lang , c2000.
Description: x, 225 p.; 24 cm.
ISBN: 0820449083 (alk. paper)
Notes: Includes bibliographical
references (p. [211]-219) and
index.
Subjects: Charter schools--United
States--Case studies. Education--
Parent participation--United
States--Case studies. Schools--
Decentralization--United States--
Case studies.
Series: Counterpoints (New York,
N.Y.); v. 135.
Variant Series: Counterpoints; v.
135
LC Classification: LB2806.36
.Y25 2000
Dewey Class No.: 371.01 21

AUTHOR INDEX

TITLE INDEX

SUBJECT INDEX

A

B

C

W